The *Titanic* and the *Lusitania*: The Controversial History of the 20th Century's Most Famous Maritime Disasters

By Charles River Editors

The *Lusitania*

About Charles River Editors

Charles River Editors provides superior editing and original writing services across the digital publishing industry, with the expertise to create digital content for publishers across a vast range of subject matter. In addition to providing original digital content for third party publishers, we also republish civilization's greatest literary works, bringing them to new generations of readers via ebooks.

Sign up here to receive updates about free books as we publish them, and visit Our Kindle Author Page to browse today's free promotions and our most recently published Kindle titles.

Introduction

The *Titanic*

The *Titanic* on April 10, 1912

"I cannot imagine any condition which would cause a ship to founder. I cannot conceive of any vital disaster happening to this vessel." – Captain Edward J. Smith

"The appearance of safety was mistaken for safety itself." – Walter Lord, author of *A Night to Remember*

"Titanic started a voyage through history when it sailed away. One century later, there is still no port at sight." - Marina Tavares Dias

Just before midnight on April 14, 1912, the RMS *Titanic*, the largest ship in the world, hit an iceberg, starting a chain of events that would ultimately make it history's most famous, and notorious, ship. In the over 100 years since it sank on its maiden voyage, the *Titanic* has been the subject of endless fascination, as evidenced by the efforts to find its final resting spot, the museums full of its objects, and the countless books, documentaries, and movies made about the doomed ocean liner. Thanks to the dramatization of the *Titanic*'s sinking and the undying interest in the story, millions of people are familiar with various aspects of the ship's demise, and the nearly 1,500 people who died in the North Atlantic in the early morning hours of April 15, 1912. The sinking of the ship is still nearly as controversial now as it was over 100 years ago, and the drama is just as compelling.

The *Titanic* was neither the first nor last big ship to sink, so it's clear that much of its appeal stems from the nature of ship itself. Indeed, the *Titanic* stands out not just for its end but for its beginning, specifically the fact that it was the most luxurious passenger ship ever built at the time. In addition to the time it took to come up with the design, the giant ship took a full three years to build, and no effort or cost was spared to outfit the *Titanic* in the most lavish ways. Given that the *Titanic* was over 100 feet tall, nearly 900 feet long, and over 90 feet wide, it's obvious that those who built her and provided all of its famous amenities had plenty of work to do. The massive ship was carrying thousands of passengers and crew members, each with their own experiences on board, and the various amenities offered among the different classes of passengers ensured that life on some decks of the ship was quite different than life on others.

Almost everyone is familiar with what happened to the *Titanic* during its maiden voyage and the tragedy that followed, but the construction of the *Titanic* is often overlooked, despite being an amazing story itself, one that combined comfort and raw power with the world's foremost technological advances. Nonetheless, the seeds of the *Titanic*'s destruction were sown even before it left for its first and last journey.

Similarly, the drama involved with the sinking of the *Titanic* often obscures the important aftermath of the disaster, particularly the several investigations conducted on both sides of the Atlantic that sought to figure out not only why the *Titanic* sank but future changes that could be made in order to protect ships and passengers in the future. In fact, the course of the investigations was interesting in itself, especially since the British and Americans reached wildly different conclusions about what went wrong and led to the ship's demise.

Naturally, the intense interest in the *Titanic* also meant that there would be great efforts made to locate the wreck. In fact, the first searches for the wreck began in the days after the giant ship went down, but given how far down it sank to the floor of the Atlantic and the fact that the ship had inaccurately transmitted its location shortly before it sank, initial efforts were doomed. As it turned out, the most famous wreck in the world would not be located until 1985, over 70 years after the ship sank that fateful April night. Since that time, underwater exploration has also helped to solve some of the mysteries surrounding the sinking of the *Titanic*, and the salvaging of countless objects and artifacts have allowed people in museums across the world to step back in time and imagine what it was like aboard history's most famous ship.

The Sinking of the *Lusitania*

A 1915 painting depicting the sinking of the *Lusitania*

"The sounds of that awe-inspiring requiem that vibrated o'er the ocean have been drowned in the waters of the deep, the instruments that gave them birth are silenced as the harps were silenced on the willow tree, but if the melody that was rehearsed could only reverberate through this land 'Nearer, My God, to Thee,' and its echoes could be heard in these halls of legislation, and at every place where our rulers and representatives pass judgment and enact and administer laws, and at every home and fireside, from the mansions of the rich to the huts and hovels of the poor, and if we could be made to feel that there is a divine law of obedience and of adjustment, and of compensation that should demand our allegiance, far above the laws that we formulate in this presence, then, from the gloom of these fearful hours we shall pass into the dawn of a higher service and of a better day, and then, Mr. President, the lives that went down upon this fated night did not go down in vain." – Senator Isidor Rayner

In 1906, the RMS *Lusitania* was at the forefront of transatlantic shipping. Briefly the largest ship in the world, the designers and engineers who built the *Lusitania* aimed for her to represent the height of luxury for passengers while also being the harbinger of a new technological age, replete with revolutionary engines that would allow the gigantic ship to move at speeds that would have been considered impossible just years earlier. Indeed, the highly competitive industry would spur the development of bigger and better ocean liners in the coming years, the most famous being the *Titanic*.

The *Lusitania* and the *Titanic* would become the two most famous ships of the early 20th century for tragic reasons, but the circumstances could not have been more different. While the *Titanic* is still notorious for being the world's best ocean liner at the time of its collision with an iceberg in 1912, the *Lusitania*'s role as a popular ocean liner has been almost completely obscured by the nature of its sinking by a German U-boat in 1915. The Germans aimed to disrupt trade by the Allied forces, but they did not have the naval forces capable of seizing merchant ships and detaining them. Furthermore, the Germans rightly suspected that the British and Americans were using passenger liners and merchant ships to smuggle weaponry across the Atlantic, but since their sole edge in the Atlantic was their fleet of submarines, the Germans had no way of confirming their suspicions, short of sinking a ship and seeing if a detonation onboard suggested the presence of munitions and gunpowder.

The Germans targeted many British merchant ships, but on May 7, 1915, a German U-boat controversially torpedoed the *Lusitania*, which sank less than 20 minutes after being struck. The attack killed over 1,000 people, including over 100 American civilians, infuriating the United States. After sinking the ship, the Germans immediately claimed that the boat was carrying "contraband of war" and was in a war zone, charges vehemently denied by the United States and the British. For awhile, the Germans tightened restrictions on their use of U-boats to placate the Americans and seek to keep them out of the war (though the restrictions would not last).

The sinking of the Lusitania in 1915 was the first major event that shifted public opinion in the United States, and support for joining the war began to rise across the country. Many Americans joined the "Preparedness Movement," which advocated at least preparing for war if not entering the war outright, and though the country would not declare war against Germany for two more years, the sinking of the *Lusitania* is still cited as a key event that set America on the path toward joining the war.

Given the importance of its sinking, debate over whether the *Lusitania* was carrying explosive munitions has raged on ever since. When the U-boat's torpedo hit the *Lusitania* and exploded, a second explosion followed the first explosion shortly after, and the Germans cited the second explosion as evidence that the torpedo had hit weapons munitions that ignited the second explosion, a charge that was strongly denied by the British. It would take multiple investigations, declassified documents, and even dives to the wreckage to determine whether the *Lusitania* was smuggling arms, and whether such munitions triggered the second explosion.

The Titanic and the Lusitania: The Controversial History of the 20th Century's Most Famous Maritime Disasters chronicles the construction and destruction of two of the most famous ships in history. Along with pictures of important people, places, and events, you will learn about the sinking of both like never before.

The *Titanic* and the *Lusitania*: The Controversial History of the 20th Century's Most Famous Maritime Disasters

About Charles River Editors

Introduction

The Titanic

   The Best and the Last of a Golden Age

   Life on the High Seas

   The Ship's Final Hours

   Among the Living and the Dead

   Investigation, Blame and Prevention

   Lost and Found

   Following the Money to Oblivion?

The Lusitania

   The Largest Ship in the World

   The Start of World War I

   Bound for Liverpool

   "A Million-Ton Hammer"

   Abandoning Ship

   Total Loss

   Certain Statements

   Online Resources

   Further Reading

Free Books by Charles River Editors

Discounted Books by Charles River Editors

The Titanic

The Best and the Last of a Golden Age

"If you enter Belfast Harbor early in the morning on the mail steamer from Fleetwood you will see far ahead of you a smudge of smoke. At first it is nothing but the apex of a great triangle formed by the heights on one side, the green wooded shores on the other, and the horizon astern. As you go on the triangle becomes narrower, the blue waters smoother, and the ship glides on in a triangle of her own a triangle of white foam that is parallel to the green triangle of the shore. Behind you the Copeland Lighthouse keeps guard over the sunrise and the tumbling surges of the Channel, before you is the cloud of smoke that joins the narrowing shores like a gray canopy; and there is no sound but the rush of foam past the ship's side." – Filson Young, *Titanic*

Most of the English speaking world is familiar with the tragic story of the *RMS Titanic*, the supposedly unsinkable luxury liner that sank on her maiden voyage, snuffing out the lives of more than 1,500 people. What many do not realize, however, is that the loss of the *Titanic* signaled more than just the loss of a large ship. It marked the end of an era, of a time when it seemed for many that life would go on as placidly as it always had, that the sun would never set on the British Empire and that the boom of prosperity brought about by the Second Industrial Revolution would last forever.

It was, in many ways, a glorious time, full of the promise of new opportunities. The *Titanic* itself, along with similar ocean liners, was a microcosm of those opportunities for, on the upper decks of the ship, just as in the upper reaches of society, were the newly wealthy, with old money rubbing shoulders with new, the Astors with members of powerful English families. Below them, in rank and location, were the middle classes, a growing breed in Europe, made up of businessmen and inventors whose efforts were fueling the western world's growing prosperity. Finally, in the lowest reaches of the ship were those who were the poorest, most of whom had saved for years to finally make their way to America, the land of opportunity. Tragically, most of them would never make it there.

Of course, the *Titanic* itself was a major part of this new and burgeoning economy, as the White Star Line cobbled together a group of wealthy investors interested in financing its construction along with that of its sister ship, the *Olympic*. The father of these plans was a man named J. Bruce Ismay, chairman of the White Star Line. Ismay worked closely with the famous American financier, J. P. Morgan to get the two ships built. They were designed to be part of the White Star Line's new *Olympic* Class and, while her sister carried the class' name, *Titanic* was named after the Titans of ancient Greek mythology. *Titanic* means "gigantic" and both ships were certainly that.

J. Bruce Ismay

In fact, *Titanic* and *Olympic* were so big that the White Star Line's construction company, Harland & Wolff had to create a new space in Belfast Harbor to build the ships, setting aside three normal sized berths to handle the project. In order to facilitate their completion, it was decided that the two vessels would be built at the same time, with crews working side by side and able to share ideas and machinery. The man charged with making the dream a reality was Irish born naval architect Thomas Andrews, a 20 year veteran of Harland &Wolff. He worked for two years on the ships, bringing to the projects a true love for all things engineering. Ultimately, he gave his life for the project, going down with *Titanic* when she sank. One contemporary said of Andrews: "When I first knew Mr. Andrews, he was a young man, but young as he was, to him were entrusted the most important and responsible duties—the direct supervision of constructing the largest ships built in the Yard from the laying of their keels until their sailing from Belfast. Such a training eminently fitted him for the important possible to which he succeeded in 1905, that of the Chief of the Designing department. For one so young, the position involved duties that taxed him to the full. To superintend the construction of ships like the *Baltic* and the *Oceanic* was a great achievement, but at the age of thirty-two to be the

Chief of a department designing leviathans like the *Olympic* was a greater one still. How well he rose to the call everyone knows. No task was too heavy, and none too light for him to grapple with successfully. He seemed endowed with boundless energy, and his interest in his work was unceasing."

A picture of the RMS *Olympic* finishing its maiden voyage in New York City in 1911

As the ships took shape in the harbor, they evolved from welded steel skeletons that ran the entire length of their respective oversized berths, into steel plated hulls six stories tall. As anyone who has read extensively on the *Titanic* knows, its most important practical feature was its fifteen bulkheads. These were supposed to make the ship unsinkable by allowing a single large hole to be sealed off and prevented from flooding the rest of the ship. Because of these bulkheads, the designers did not think it necessary to provide the ships with the standard double hulls that most of the ships of that day featured.

The *Titanic* was a source of pride for those who worked on it. One worker's granddaughter said, "*Titanic* was always part of our family lore. I have a hexagonal marquetry chessboard at home, which we always called the *Titanic* chessboard. It was a Harland and Wolff 'homer', a beautiful piece of craftsmanship made from lovely old pieces of wood brought home from the shipyard, mounted on a cheap piece of pine. We learned to play draughts on it as children, and to me it's a physical connection with *Titanic*. There must be so many families that have bits and pieces connected to *Titanic*, all kinds of treasures that are worth nothing in monetary terms but which connect local people to *Titanic* and the shipyard. … What happened to *Titanic* was a disaster, she herself was not. And *Titanic* was not the end of the Harland and Wolff shipyard. It continued for years afterwards … Here in Northern Ireland, you can take the story of *Titanic* into any school, and there will always be someone who pipes up that their great-great-grandfather worked on the ship. It's a story that cuts across the religious and political divide."

Pictures of the Titanic being built

The site of the construction

The *Titanic* and *Olympic* both under construction side by side

Picture of a man posing next to the Titanic's stern and rudder

When *Titanic*'s exterior was completed, more than 10,000 people gathered at the harbor on May 31, 1911 to see her launched. Ironically, those in charge opted to forego the normal christening ceremony and instead simply watched quietly as the ship, riding on twenty-two tons of soap and tallow, slid into the ocean. From there, she was towed to a new berth, where she would remain for the eleven months that it would take to complete her interior. Her massive engines and giant propeller would only be used later, when she officially got underway.

Picture of the 1911 launch of the *Titanic*

When they were ultimately pressed into action, *Titanic*'s three engines would surely impress everyone around, for they were built to be among the fastest of that generation. Each was more than 20 feet tall and 15 feet across and was powered by 29 boilers that provided the energy it needed to turn the propeller it was attached to. The boilers in turn were powered by more than 1400 gallons of water heated by 150 furnaces that were designed to use 8,000 tons of coal on *Titanic's* first Atlantic crossing.

Of course, most of these details were lost on *Titanic*'s passengers, who, like cruisers of today, were much more interested in the comfort of their quarters than in what was moving them to their destination. The builders knew this, and poured much of their efforts into designing and building the ship's most attractive features. Someone would later call *Titanic* "the ship of dreams" and to most of her passengers it was indeed that.

Of the six decks on the *Titanic*, the top one was known as the Boat Deck because it was the center of the ship's navigation and sailing abilities. Only the wealthiest and most important passengers would come aboard the ship via the Boat Deck. From there, they would likely head downstairs to A Deck, which housed the most elegant spaces on the ship and featured sumptuous wood paneling, soft, deep carpets and crystal chandeliers. Below A Deck was B Deck, the location of many of the First Class staterooms, as well as many of the ship's offices. Like C Deck, A and B Decks extended the entire length of the ship. However, its similarities ended there, as C Deck featured gears to raise and lower the anchors, as well as a special dining hall set aside for those men who worked stoking the ship's fires. D Deck was the first "short deck" and held the firemen's quarters at one end of the ship, with more First Class staterooms at the other end. E Deck housed the crew and steerage passengers, along with a few more First and Second Class rooms, as well as the Turkish Baths. Below E Deck were more rooms for Third Class passengers, as well as luggage rooms, a post office and a racquet ball court.

Picture of the top deck

Pictures of the B Deck

   Several of these floors were joined by *Titanic*'s most spectacular interior feature, her Grand Staircase. It was, in fact, two staircases that began on opposite sides of the Boat Deck and allowed its passengers to descend gracefully to E Deck, by which time the two had joined to share a center railing. From there, they could take one more flight down to F Deck. Today, the Grand Staircase continues to serve as an entry point to the ship for those deep sea scientists exploring the vessel.

A depiction of the Grand Staircase in a booklet designed by White Star Line

Picture of the Grand Staircase on the *Olympic*, similar to what was on the *Titanic*

Needless to say, those working to create the dream that was *Titanic* often found themselves with conflicting ideas on what was important. For instance, Andrews placed a high priority on using the best materials possible in every important part of the ship. While many at Harland & Wolff agreed with him, others, including Ismay, felt that passengers would rather have large spaces with better views of the ocean. Between them, those involved arrived at two separate conclusions that would forevermore shape *Titanic*'s future.

The first issue they addressed badly concerned the number of lifeboats the ship was to carry. This now infamous decision was made at a time when there were no hard and fast rules concerning such matters, and when each shipping company was trusted to make wise choices for the safety of its passengers. For its part, the White Star Line considered *Titanic* to be "its own lifeboat" and therefore cut back the number of lifeboats from sixty-four to twenty. While this decision has been condemned for more than a century, it is only fair to note that no one imagined that, even if it were to sink, any ship of *Titanic*'s size would go down too fast. Because the

North Atlantic was a busy and popular shipping lane, the assumption was that another ship would arrive to safely offload passengers in an emergency, long before anyone would even get their feet wet.

Some of the *Titanic*'s lifeboats in New York after the ship sank

The second bad decision that was made during those early days of *Titanic*'s construction concerned the all-important bulkheads themselves. Andrews emphasized to those around him that they had to be high enough to remain above the waterline in case of an emergency. However, Ismay disagreed and insisted that they go no higher than D Deck, partly so that the First Class Dining Room could be made larger. There was also no provision made to seal the tops of the bulkheads in such a way that water rushing into one could not overflow into another.

Among the most cutting edge aspects of *Titanic*'s design was the use throughout the ship of electricity, still a new convenience. In fact, the ship was dependent on electrically powered lights, fans, signals and communication devices in a way that no earlier ship had been. These features were powered by four separate engines and dynamos that allowed many of the lights aboard the ship to remain burning even after they were underwater. The ship's lavatories also featured hot and cold running water.

Still, one of the most impressive features on the ship was its state of the art communication system. The ship's radio room featured two spark-gap wireless telegraphs that passengers and crew alike could use to send messages. The former would, of course, have to pay a substantial price for this convenience. Those wishing to communicate with others across the length of the large ship could use any number of telephones placed around the vessel. Again, these were primarily for the use of the ship's crew and only the occasional First Class passenger.

Life on the High Seas

Pictures of the *Titanic* being tugged from Belfast for her trials at sea

"All afternoon we steamed along the coast of Ireland, with grey cliffs guarding the shores, and hills rising behind gaunt and barren; as dusk fell, the coast rounded away from us to the northwest, and the last we saw of Europe was the Irish mountains dim and faint in the dropping darkness. With the thought that we had seen the last of land until we set foot on the shores of America, I retired to the library to write letters, little knowing that many things would happen to us all—many experiences, sudden, vivid and impressive to be encountered, many perils to be faced, many good and true people for whom we should have to mourn—before we saw land again.: - Lawrence Beesley

On Wednesday, April 10, 1912, after less than a week of sea trials, *Titanic* began to take on her first passengers. That day, around 400 crewmen and staff members spent hours helping her 1,200 passengers find their rooms, store or unpack their luggage and bid farewell to their loved ones. Except for the Marconi men who ran the telegraphs, they all ultimately worked for 63 year old Captain Edward John Smith. He was the oldest officer aboard and the product of a long career at sea. He was anticipating an exciting but safe voyage to his destination.

Perhaps not surprisingly, some people who didn't have tickets tried to get on. English teacher

Lawrence Beesley explained, "A knot of stokers ran along the quay, with their kit slung over their shoulders in bundles, and made for the gangway with the evident intention of joining the ship. But a petty officer guarding the shore end of the gangway firmly refused to allow them on board; they argued, gesticulated, apparently attempting to explain the reasons why they were late, but he remained obdurate and waved them back with a determined hand. The gangway was dragged back amid their protests, putting a summary ending to their determined efforts to join the *Titanic*."

A picture of Beesley in the gymnasium

Of the 1,200 passengers, 322 were travelling First Class while 275 had Second Class accommodations. Among those traveling Second Class were some who could have easily afforded the £870 First Class accommodations but did not get the tickets in time. Not surprisingly, there was plenty of competition among those who enjoyed pleasure cruising to make the famous maiden voyage on the *Titanic*. The rest of the passengers were travelling in steerage and though the accommodations were far from luxurious, they would enjoy much better conditions than those traveling under similar circumstances just thirty years earlier.

   Once the ship weighed anchor at Southampton, she sailed across the English Channel to the small coastal community of Cherbourg, where she anchored for the night before beginning her real voyage. This short trip gave the crew a chance to get to know the ship better before putting out to sea. Part of their duties included becoming accustomed to *Titanic*'s capacity for speed. Smith, anxious to make the most of this "shake down" voyage, hoped to push his engines enough to get to his American destination a bit early.

The *Titanic* at the Southampton docks ahead of her maiden voyage

An advertisement for the *Titanic*

One of the workers on the Titanic remembered how lovely the scene was around England: "We dropped down Spithead, past the shores of the Isle of Wight looking superbly beautiful in new spring foliage, exchanged salutes with a White Star tug lying-to in wait for one of their liners inward bound, and saw in the distance several warships with attendant black destroyers guarding the entrance from the sea. In the calmest weather we made Cherbourg just as it grew dusk and left again about 8.30, after taking on board passengers and mail. We reached Queenstown about 12 noon on Thursday, after a most enjoyable passage across the Channel, although the wind was almost too cold to allow sitting out on deck on Thursday morning. The coast of Ireland looked very beautiful as we approached Queenstown Harbor, the brilliant morning sun showing up the green hillsides and picking out groups of dwellings dotted here and there above the rugged grey cliffs that fringed the coast."

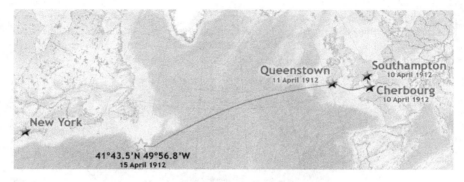

The route of the maiden voyage

The *Titanic* at Cork Harbor on April 11, 1912

In addition to taking walks and enjoying the pleasant weather, those sailing on *Titanic* also had plenty of time to relax and write letters, a popular pastime of the day, especially for those traveling. These letters could be written on the ship's elegant stationary and posted on board ship. They would then be passed off to other vessels that *Titanic* might come in contact with during her trip.

While the First and Second Class passengers were segregated from each other in their suites, one amenity that they did share was the ship's elevators, which were attended at all times by a uniformed operator. Again, comfort would later turn to tragedy when the elevator shafts themselves proved to be conduits that allowed the water rushing in from the damaged ship to quickly travel to its upper floors.

In addition to these smaller amenities, *Titanic* featured a well-appointed gymnasium that included a punching bag, rowing machine, several exercise bikes, a squash court, and the largest swimming pool on any ship at that time, complete with a diving board. There was also a Turkish Bath and a steam room and several heated baths.

Picture of the gymnasium in 1912

A depiction of the gymnasium in a booklet designed by White Star Line

Of course, all that exercise, as well as long walks along the deck, allowed *Titanic*'s passengers to work up quite an appetite. This problem could be easily solved at any of the ship's several restaurants. The most elegant of these was "The Ritz" and was open only to First Class passengers. It featured an a la carte menu and sported Axminster carpets, small private tables, and huge windows that looked out onto the surrounding sea. While waiting to make their grand entrance into the Ritz, passengers could relax in the large reception room outside the restaurant. Most would recognize this antechamber as the first place they had gone through when entering the ship. The largest restaurant on the ship was the First Class Dining Saloon, which covered much of D Deck and seated up to more than 500 people. There was also a Second Class Dining Saloon that shared its kitchen. Two Cafés, the Verandah and the Parisien, were open to both First and Second Class passengers and opened onto the Promenade Deck.

Picture of the Parisien on the *Titanic*

Picture of the Verandah on the *Olympic*, similar to the one on the *Titanic*

Picture of the First Class Dining Saloon on *Olympic*, similar to the one on *Titanic*

Just as there were certain spaces on the ship that were segregated by social standing and finances, so there were areas on the *Titanic* that were segregated by gender. Among these was the smoking room, which was open only to men; in fact, only to men with First Class tickets. First Class passenger Major Arthur Peuchen remembered, "Sunday evening I dined with my friends, Markleham Molson, Mr. Allison, and Mrs. Allison and their daughter was there for a short time. The dinner was an exceptionally good dinner. It seemed to be a better bill of fare than usual, although they are all good. After dinner my friends and I went to the sitting-out room and had some coffee. I left the friends I had dined with about 9 o'clock, I think, or a little later. I then went up to the smoking room and joined Mr. Beatty, Mr. McCaffry, and another English gentleman who was going to Canada. We sat chatting and smoking there until probably twenty minutes after eleven, or it may have been a little later than that."

Those traveling in First and Second Class enjoyed delicacies such as Fillets of Brill, Grilled Mutton Chops, Potted Shrimps, Galantine of Chicken and Apple Meringue, all on fine china. Those travelling in First Class dressed formally for the seven course dinner each evening, while Second Class passengers had to make do with four courses. Both groups enjoyed the music provided by the ship's own eight piece orchestra. Even those in steerage enjoyed the rare pleasure of dining three times a day on meals prepared by someone else and served on crisp linen tablecloths. On the other hand, those

Before or after dinner, passengers in First and Second Class could make use of *Titanic*'s well stocked library. Not only did it provide interesting books, but it also gave those traveling a chance to interact with other people with similar interests. The library became even more popular as the ship travelled north and the weather became less pleasant. At the same time, the area outside the library became something of a makeshift playroom for children in the upper classes, who were usually accompanied there by their nannies or other caregivers.

While the children of the wealthiest passengers might have needed a space in which to run around and play, their parents were likely perfectly content to remain in their elegant rooms, each designed in its own style. Thus, a Louis XVI stateroom might exist side by side with one decorated in the Queen Anne style and across from another room with Italian Renaissance features. The two finest suites on the ship were located on B Deck and included two bedrooms, each with its own dressing room, a sitting room, a private bathroom and a small room suitable for a lady's maid or valet. Like many of the other nicest rooms, these featured an imitation coal fireplace. The Second Class rooms were nearly as nice as the standard First Class accommodations.

Naturally, single men took note of the ladies aboard. One of them recalled, "Close beside me— so near that I cannot avoid hearing scraps of their conversation—are two American ladies, both dressed in white, young, probably friends only: one has been to India and is returning by way of England, the other is a school-teacher in America, a graceful girl with a distinguished air heightened by a pair of pince-nez. Engaged in conversation with them is a gentleman whom I subsequently identified from a photograph as a well-known resident of Cambridge, Massachusetts, genial, polished, and with a courtly air towards the two ladies, whom he has known but a few hours. From time to time as they talk, a child acquaintance breaks in on their conversation and insists on their taking notice of a large doll clasped in her arms."

For those in steerage, it was another story. Instead of individual rooms, those travelling third class would share their accommodations with perfect strangers. For this reason, the two sexes were segregated, with women and young children sleeping at one end of the ship and men sleeping at the other. Each small room featured upper and lower berths for four, six or eight people. Even the dining facilities were separate, so that a man might only be able to see his wife or children in the General Room, a large, open room outfitted with small teak tables, chairs and benches, as well as a piano that anyone able to was welcome to play. The men in steerage had their own smoking room and all Third Class passengers were welcome to use the Promenade set aside for them at the rear of the ship.

People in steerage also knew how to have fun. One of the ship's workers described one scene: "Looking down astern from the Boat Deck or from B Deck to the steerage quarters, I often noticed how the third-class passengers were enjoying every minute of the time. A most uproarious skipping game of the mixed-double type was the great favorite, while 'in and out and roundabout' went a Scotchman with his bagpipes playing something that Gilbert says 'faintly resembled an air.' Standing aloof from all of them, generally on the raised stern deck above the 'playing field,' was a man of about twenty to twenty-four years of age, well-dressed, always gloved and nicely groomed, and obviously quite out of place among his fellow-passengers; he never looked happy all the time. I watched him, and classified him at hazard as the man who had been a failure in some way at home and had received the proverbial shilling plus third-class fare to America. He did not look resolute enough or happy enough to be working out his own problems. Another interesting man was travelling steerage, but had placed his wife in a second class cabin. He would climb the stairs leading from the steerage to the second deck and talk affectionately with his wife across the low gate which separated them."

For a few days, all was well and everyone went about their business. Then Sunday morning, April 14 dawned bright and cold. The captain, as was his custom, held a Morning Prayer service in the First Class Dining Saloon. Afterward, those who attended went on to enjoy a delicious lunch and then amused themselves as they thought best. One of the passengers, an Anglican minister, organized an impromptu hymn singing for the evening.

For those passengers who chose to attend, it would be one of their last happy memories of the trip. This proved to be an enjoyable time that lasted well into the evening. Captain Smith himself may have looked in on the group as he made his final tour of the ship before retiring for the night at 9:30. This was not unusual, as he trusted his crew to keep things running smoothly while he slept. It is unclear whether or not he knew about the warnings that had been arriving steadily all evening that there were icebergs in the area. Had he known of these, he might have ordered the ship to slow down, as she was travelling at 22 knots (25 miles per hour), which was nearly her top speed.

While Smith was later criticized for how fast his ship was travelling that night, it should be noted that conditions in the North Atlantic were unusually good that year and it seems unlikely that he could have anticipated such a disaster as was even then looming.

While it may seem that a quiet, still moonlit night would be ideal conditions from a visual standpoint, the opposite was actually true. The lookouts would normally expect to see waves of some sort lapping against the side of the iceberg, creating movement that would catch their attention. However, this did not happen and by the time that the lookout saw the infamous iceberg at 11:40 that fateful night, it was too late to do anything. Still, he quickly relayed the information to Quartermaster Robert Hichens, who immediately attempted to turn the ship to port side (left). However, nothing as large as the *Titanic* turns quickly and the ship's hull structure struck the iceberg again and again, creating a series of holes in the side of the ship. Though the holes were small, they were large enough to let in seawater, and that was all it took to sink her.

The Ship's Final Hours

Pictures of the iceberg that the *Titanic* is believed to have struck

"Then I run down to my cabin to bring my other clothes, watch and bag but only had time to take the watch and coat when water with enormous force came into the cabin and I had to rush up to the deck again where I found my friends standing with lifebelts on and with terror painted on their faces. What should I do now, with no lifebelt and no shoes and no cap?" – Carl Jansson, a passenger in steerage

On the night of April 14, the moonless night and the calm weather conspired to make it harder for the lookouts to see the iceberg sitting right in *Titanic*'s path around 11:40 that night. The two men had been told to "keep a sharp look-out for ice, particularly small ice and growlers," and when Fleet spotted the iceberg about twenty minutes before midnight, he phoned the bridge to report, "Iceberg, right ahead!" The message was relayed to Quartermaster Robert Hichens, who was ordered to change the ship's course to turn it to port side (left).

Frederick Fleet

Due to the ship's size and the complexities involved in making a sudden turn of direction, *Titanic* proved unable to completely miss the iceberg. The ship's speed was reduced in an effort to turn the ship, but investigators would later argue that if the ship had maintained full speed as it turned, it might have missed the iceberg altogether. In the end, the ship's side glanced across the iceberg, resulting in a series of small punctures in the hull and a bunch of ice falling onto the forward decks. Contemporaries thought the iceberg left a gash in the hull at least 300 feet long, but underwater explorations of the wreck would later determine that there were only a series of small punctures in an area of the hull that covered less than 15 square feet. The furthest distance between any of the small punctures was about 40 feet. As Robert Ballard, the man whose expeditions discovered the wreck of the *Titanic*, later put it, the notion that the holes in the hull could have been so small was discounted because nobody "could believe that the great ship was sunk by a little sliver."

Once workers began to inspect the damage, it became clear there was a major problem. As Fourth Officer Joseph Boxhall put it, "I was just approaching the bridge [on the] starboard side. ... I could not see what had occurred. ...I heard the sixth officer say what it was. He said we had struck an iceberg. ... At the time of the impact I was just coming along the deck and almost abreast of the captain's quarters, and I heard the report of three bells. ... That signifies something has been seen ahead. Almost at the same time I heard the first officer give the order 'Hard astarboard,' and the engine telegraph rang, ordering the ship's head to port. ... It seemed to me to strike the bluff of the bow. It is in the forward part of the ship, but almost on the side. It is just where the ship begins to widen out on the starboard side. ... A glancing blow. A slight impact. It did not seem to me to be very serious. I did not take it seriously. ... The captain said, 'What have we struck?' Mr. Murdoch, the first officer, said, 'We have struck an iceberg.' He followed on to say - Mr. Murdoch followed on to say, 'I put her hard astarboard and run the engines full astern, but it was too close; she hit it.' ... Mr. Murdoch also said, 'I intended to port around it. But she hit before I could do any more. The watertight doors are closed, sir.' ... I saw him close them. ... And the captain asked him if he had rung the warning bell. He said, 'Yes, sir.' ... We all walked out to the corner of the bridge then to look at the iceberg. The captain, first officer, and myself."

Though the ship was due to sink from the moment the iceberg cut the holes in her hull, most people had no idea they were in any real danger. Most of the passengers were asleep and those who were not were likely busy entertaining themselves. Even when word spread that there had been some sort of collision, few people took it seriously. The only ones who could see the damage were located far below decks, working hard away from the comfortable passengers. They were also the ones in the most immediate danger, as compartment after compartment filled with icy salt water.

The first passengers to get a sense of how serious the danger was were likely those in steerage. Some survivors would later testify of awakening to find water on the floor of their rooms. Rousting others, they began to make their way upstairs in the hopes of finding out what was going on. While much would later be made of the myth of locked doors that kept them from reaching safety, testimony given at hearings following the disaster denied that this was true. Thus, it seems likely that during the crisis the members of different classes might have indeed mingled for the first time on board.

Even as the men below decks manned the pumps in a futile attempt to keep the ship afloat a little longer, more and more people were waking up to see what was going on. The men most likely came on deck first to find out about the situation, not wanting to disturb their wives and children. Some, like the well-known author Colonel Archibald Gracie, used the time to make plans for the next day's activities. Others, such as John Jacob Astor, were a bit more concerned.

He was travelling with his pregnant young wife and was acutely sensitive to her safety and comfort. Having made his fortune by studying those around him, Astor may have been one of the first First Class passengers to be aware of the seriousness of their situation.

Unfortunately, the man who should have been in the most control seemed at first flummoxed by what was happening. Captain Smith felt around for a solution for more than half an hour, sometimes giving orders, sometimes lost in thought. However, he soon pulled himself together and began making what arrangements he could to save the lives of those entrusted to his care. By this time, the watertight doors had been closed. This would slow the water's spread but would not stop it. Smith also ordered the ship's large pumps engaged but it was too late for that, as most of them had already been swamped. Finally, he ordered that the ship's exact location be determined and that this information be telegraphed to any ship in the area that might be listening. Jack Phillips, one of the telegraph operators, would later be famous for remaining at his post, typing out signals again and again until he himself ultimately lost his life.

Second Steward Joseph Wheat later testified, "I went upstairs to E Deck again and went down to F Deck to close the bulkhead doors on F Deck by the Turkish Baths. There are two bulkhead doors there. ... I closed the inside one myself, and then to close the other, we had to go on top and turn that one with a key. Mr. Dodd and Crosby, the Turkish Bath attendant, helped me. …they are both on the starboard side. …they are closed with a key. ... I did it on my own. [Later] as I was coming up, there was water running down off E Deck onto F Deck, down our section…it had come from E Deck and was running down onto F. It was running down the stairway. Yes, the only stairway down there."

Gilbert Balfour was operating communications for the Marconi Co. on the *Baltic* and later discussed receiving *Titanic*'s distress signal: "We were just 243 miles southeast of the position of the *Titanic* when we first got her C. Q. D. call, about 11 o'clock, New York time, Sunday evening. We got the C. Q. D. call, giving his position, just saying 'Struck an iceberg,' giving his present position, and saying that he required immediate assistance. We did not acknowledge it direct then, but simply warned the bridge in the usual course; the ship turned around, and we took the first opportunity, which was a couple of minutes later, or it may have been five minutes later, to advise the Titanic that we were coming. The next we heard from her was about 10 minutes later. ... We received a message saying the *Titanic* had struck an iceberg and required immediate assistance, giving us her position, 41° 46' north, 50° 14' west. Capt. Ranson, so far as I know, was immediately called out, and about 11:08 or 11:09 the officer came down from the bridge, in the usual course, to verify the position, and to see if I had…any additional information."

The first ship to respond to *Titanic*'s pleas for help was a German vessel, the *Frankfurt*. However there was some sort of miscommunication between the two ships and the *Frankfurt* steamed on without offering aid.

While mistrust and misunderstanding prevented the *Frankfurt* from rendering assistance, the men on the *Titanic* also figured that since ships like the *Titanic* were so large and well-built, they would typically remain afloat for some time, even after a collision. Therefore, it seemed safe to wait for help from *Carpathia*, which also answered the distress call and was berthed out of England.

Harold Cottam, the telegraph operator aboard the *Carpathia*, had been up on the bridge checking in shortly before the *Titanic* sent out the distress signal, but he had turned in for the night when *Titanic* sent her first distress signal, so he missed it. Fortunately, he decided to take a minute before he went off duty to contact *Titanic* and let her know he had some messages to relay to her passengers. He later explained, "I asked him (Phillips) if he was aware that Cape Cod was sending a batch of messages for him. … He said, 'Come at once. It is a distress message; C. Q. D.' … I confirmed it by asking him if I was to report it to the captain. … Because it is always wise to confirm a message of that description."

As soon as Captain A. H. Rostron heard the message, he instructed Cottam to radio *Titanic* with *Carpathia's* position. Cottam continued, "About four minutes afterwards…we communicated with each other [and] confirmed both positions, that of the *Titanic* and ours. … A few minutes afterwards…there was another ship calling the *Titanic*. … The *Frankfurt*. … [Next] I heard the *Olympic* calling the *Titanic*. … He was calling him and offering a service message. … Nothing, for about a half a minute. Everything was quiet. … I asked the *Titanic* if he was aware that the *Olympic* was calling him, sir. He said he was not. He told me he could not read him because the rush of air and the escape of steam. … Then the *Titanic* called the *Olympic*. … I told the *Titanic* to call the *Baltic*. The communication was apparently unsatisfactory. I was in communication at regular intervals the whole of the time until the last communication gained with the *Titanic*. He told him to come at once; that he was head down. And he sent his position."

By this time, the passengers on *Titanic* had been awakened and ordered to dress warmly, don their life vests and report to the Boat Deck. Needless to say, these instructions, coming in the middle of a frosty night, were alarming to many. However, the crew worked hard to reassure the passengers that all was well, implying to many that this was just an extra precaution. Unfortunately, the words were soon drowned out by the cries of those who had seen water rising in the ship's hallways.

Meanwhile, some of the passengers remarked to each other that there was a light in the distance, likely that of an approaching ship coming to lend its aid. However, the light soon disappeared as the *California*, ignoring the distress flares she saw and unaware of what was happening so close to her, sailed on by. She would return some hours later to help, but too late for many who might otherwise have been rescued.

At around this time, Captain Smith gave the order that the lifeboats should be uncovered and prepared for boarding. Even this proved to be a problem because the crew was still new to the ship and unaware of what their actual duties were during a time of crisis. Thus, something as simple as better training and a lifeboat drill at the beginning of the voyage might have made the difference between life and death for many on board that night. Instead, the first lifeboats were sent out with far fewer people aboard than the sixty-five they were designed to hold. Part of what hampered them in their efforts was the passenger's own beliefs that nothing could sink such a large ship. Therefore, they were initially unwilling to be lowered down the tall, well lit side to the murky darkness below.

    Then there was the question of who should be allowed on the boats themselves. Some crewmen maintained a "women and children" first policy, prohibiting men from entering the boats at all. Others allowed anyone coming to their stations to board the boats. As a result, while wives were tearfully being pulled from their husbands' arms on one side of the ship, wealthy bachelors were stepping into safety on the other side. This would later add to the scandal of what happened that night.

Illustrations depicting wives staying with their husbands or parting with them

As bad as loading the lifeboats was, lowering them was even worse, as men unfamiliar with the mechanisms controlling the boats tried to lower them steadily down a height of dozens of feet while those in the boats shook with terror. One boat was very nearly lowered right on top of another while the block and tackle system jammed on another boat, nearly dumping its passengers out.

A depiction of Lifeboat 15 being lowered nearly onto Lifeboat 13

Once a boat was safely in the water, the question arose as to what to do next. Some felt they should stay near the ship in case there was actually no crisis. Others felt that they should row far away in order not to be dragged under by the suction when she went down. Some lifeboats were properly equipped with flashlights and food and water while others had nothing on board to support survival. Emily Ryerson later testified, "Then we turned to pick up some of those in the water. Some of the women protested, but others persisted, and we dragged in six or seven men; the men we rescued were principally stokers, stewards, sailors, etc., and were so chilled and frozen already they could hardly move. Two of them died in the stern later and many were raving and moaning and delirious most of the time. We had no lights or compass. There were several babies in the boat, but there was no milk or water. (I believe these were all stowed away somewhere, but no one knew where, and as the bottom of the boat was full of water and the boat full of people, it was very difficult to find anything.)"

Ultimately, however, all these memories would pale in comparison to the ultimate terrible sight of that night, the moment when the ship itself finally sank. So traumatic was this memory that for years eyewitnesses would disagree on what they saw. Some would say that the mighty ship just slipped quietly under the waves while others would insist that her hull rose high into the air before breaking off and sinking in two separate pieces. Others would claim they heard an explosion while still others maintained that it was silent, with only the sound of the water rushing back into place on the surface, having consumed its steel and iron meal. Whatever happened, it was over quickly, at 2:20 AM, just two hours and forty minutes after the mighty ship hit the towering iceberg.

One passenger described the scene to investigators: "After the *Titanic* sank, we saw no lights and no one seemed to know what direction to take. Lowe, the officer in charge of the boat, had called out earlier for all to tie together. So we now heard his whistle, and as soon as we could make out the other boats in the dark, five of us were tied together, and we drifted about without rowing, as the sea was calm, waiting for the dawn. It was very cold, and soon a breeze sprang up, and it was hard to keep our heavy boat bow on, but as the cries died down, we could see dimly what seemed to be a raft with about twenty men standing on it, back to back. It was the overturned boat and as the sailors on our boat said we could still carry eight or ten more people, we called for another boat to volunteer and go to rescue them. So we two cut loose our painters and between us got all the men off. They were nearly gone and could not have held out much longer."

An illustration of the *Titanic* sinking made on the *Carpathia* and based on Jack Thayer's description

Among the Living and the Dead

"Sinking of the Titanic" by Henry Reuterdahl

"In no instance, I am happy to say, did I hear any word of rebuke from a swimmer because of a refusal to grant assistance... [one refusal] was met with the manly voice of a powerful man... 'All right boys, good luck and God bless you.'" – Archibald Gracie

Decades would pass before anyone knew what happened to the ship after it was gone from sight. This, however, was the least of the worries of the more than 1,000 people who she sent into the freezing water. Many of them would drown immediately while most would slowly succumb to hypothermia in the minutes that followed. All were surrounded on all sides by oil and refuse from the broken ship and those who survived were able to do so only by finding some way to raise themselves out of the icy water.

One of the strangest stories to be told by a survivor was that of Rosa Abbott, who lost both of her children when the ship's boiler exploded as the vessel sank. Ironically, it was this explosion that likely saved her life, as it warmed the water around her and bought her the additional minutes needed to survive until she was rescued. Like Thomas Dillon, another of a handful of survivors who were pulled from the water, she was surrounded on all sides by the screams and pleading of those less fortunate ones who were slowly freezing to death before her very eyes.

In general, their pleas initially went unanswered by those in the lifeboats, who were afraid that they themselves would be swamped if they returned to the desperate victims. At the same time, most of those suffering remained invisible, just pleading voices swallowed up in the black darkness. Many of those who made it aboard a collapsible lifeboat still perished in the cold, their dead bodies lowered back into the water to make room to pick up living victims. Then there were those who lost sight of the other boats and feared they would be lost forever in that dark night.

The overturned collapsible Lifeboat B

Fortunately, this at least would not be the case, for by the time the *Titanic* slipped out of sight, the *Carpathia* and another ship, the *Baltic*, were steaming toward the survivors. The *Carpathia* was closer and arrived first, making Captain Rostron the hero of the day. A slave to efficiency, he had everything organized for a speedy rescue by the time he arrived at the scene. In addition to ordering his crew to prepare to care for the injured and those in shock, he made plans to control the way in which the world would learn of the tragedy, thus doing his best to spare the feelings of those with loved ones aboard the ship. Most of all, he reminded his own men to be vigilant in looking out for more icebergs.

The *Carpathia*

Rostron

A picture of Lifeboat 6 approaching the *Carpathia*

A picture of Lifeboat D approaching the *Carpathia*

Some of the lifeboats aboard the *Carpathia*

His biggest concern, of course, was how to get all of the survivors onto the *Carpathia* from wherever they were at the time of his arrival. Until he arrived at the site, he believed he was going to be transferring passengers from the still floating *Titanic*. Therefore he had his own lifeboats prepared for this purpose. In order to keep the hopes up of those he was coming for, he ordered his men to fire a new flare into the air every fifteen minutes, allowing those waiting to see the help was indeed coming.

The *Carpathia* finally arrived at the scene at 4:00 AM on Monday, April 15. Looking out for a distressed ship, the crew was shocked to instead find a sea of dead and dying people, along with a handful of partially loaded lifeboats. They immediately swung into action, lowering lifeboats to move among those in the water and try to pull in those who were still alive. As the sun rose that morning, though, it soon revealed the awful truth; there were very few people left alive in the water.

In the end, Rostron and his crew, "got thirteen lifeboats alongside, two emergency boats, two Berthon boats. There was one lifeboat which we saw was abandoned, and one of the Berthon boats, of course, was not launched from the ship, I understand…one that was capsized. That was in the wreckage. That was the twenty." While he knew instinctively that he needed to take these boats back to New York with him, Rostron was still concerned about what to do with all of them. However, he soon came up with a plan: "As the people came out, we left the boats alongside. Of course lots of gear had been knocked out of the boats and thrown out of the way of the people as they were getting up; so, while they were holding this service and while I was cruising around, I had all of my boats swung out, ready for lowering over, and while they were getting all the people aboard from the boats, I got the spare men and some of my officers, and swung my boats inboard again, and landed them on their blocks and secured them, and swung the davits out again, disconnected the falls again, and got up the *Titanic's* boats. While I was cruising around, I was also getting these boats up. I got seven of the *Titanic's* boats up in our davits, and six up on the forecastle head with the forward derricks; so that is thirteen boats in all."

Once aboard the *Carpathia*, those still conscious began their terrible search for their loved ones. While there were a few happy reunions, there were many more mourners, for very few of those not in lifeboats survived the night's terrible ordeal. Conscious of everyone's raw feelings, Rostron ordered a prayer service be held for those who had been picked up. This served the dual purpose of providing comfort for the survivors and keeping them below decks while he and his crew continued their increasingly futile search for survivors. However, *Carpathia* did not remain at this task long, instead turning it over to the *Baltic* and the *Californian*, both of which arrived on the scene later in the day. As soon as they were on site, Rostron turned his attention to getting the survivors to their original destination, New York City, as soon as possible. He did this even though it would delay his own arrival in Halifax, Nova Scotia, his destination.

As was alluded to earlier, one of the biggest challenges facing Rostron as he steamed toward land was how to control the information concerning what had happened, both on his own ship and in the press. Even before their clothes were dry, some of *Titanic*'s passengers began to speculate that they had somehow been the victims of foul play, most likely at the hands of Germany. Rostron knew that there would be plenty of investigations in the future and was anxious not to stir up emotions unnecessarily.

Captain Rostron would later testify, "Daylight was breaking just as we were taking the passengers up from the first boat. By the time we got them on board, there was sufficient daylight for us to see the boats in the immediate vicinity of the ship. It must have been a quarter of an hour after I got them all on board that I saw the other boats. It was not sufficiently light to see the other boats. They were within a range of four or five miles. …it was getting lighter all the time. Daylight broke very quickly, and we picked them up here and there within a range of four or five miles, as I say. Several of the boats could have accommodated a good many more people, and two or three boats were rather crowded, I thought. The only wreckage we saw there was very small stuff - a few deck chairs and pieces of cork from lifebelts, and a few lifebelts knocking about, and things of that description, all very small stuff indeed. There was very little indeed. We only saw one body. When we got up to the wreckage, it would be about twenty minutes to eight, or a quarter to eight, or something like that. We had not seen this wreckage. We had been dodging about picking up the other boats. I had not any idea where the wreckage was. As soon as we had finished taking the passengers from the boats, I cleared off to another boat to pick them up, and was dodging about all over the place to pick them up. It was only when we got to the last boat that we got close up to the wreckage. It was close up to the wreckage. It would be about a quarter to eight when we got there."

Then there was the matter of dealing with the press. Not surprisingly, many of those on board wanted to contact their relatives and let them know what had happened. However, Rostron, knowing the notorious yellow-press of the era would be hungry for a story, allowed little ship to shore communication. One of the few messages sent was that of Bruce Ismay, who cabled his superiors at the White Star Line that the ship had gone down. He would spend much of the rest of his life answering for his own survival in the face of the tragedy. Rostron's problem was complicated by the fact that there were a number of very prominent people aboard the *Titanic*, including Major Archibald Willingham Butt, a military aide to the President of the United States, William Howard Taft. The White House itself soon cabled him for information on Butts, who had in fact perished.

By the time *Carpathia* arrived in New York on Friday, April 19, 1912, the city was in a frenzy of curiosity and excitement. The ship was immediately inundated with everyone from curious reporters to prying politicians to fearful family members, all desperate for news about the disaster. Not surprisingly, this led to an explosion of misinformation and mistrust. Of course, it didn't help that the accurate news was mostly bad. Grief spread across both Great Britain and America like the oil stick still floating above where the ship had gone down. While many began to arrange funerals and memorial services, a few others made their way back to the site, hoping to find some answers about what exactly had gone wrong. Among those travelling in that dreadful week was the ship's doctor for the *Minia*. Examining the bodies that the ship had picked up, he was the first to determine that hypothermia had taken so many lives.

In all, about 1,500 people lost their lives that night, more than twice as many as survived. Most of the children in First and Second Class made it to land safely but more than 70% of the crewmen, including the captain, went down with the ship.

At first, those caught in grief formed irrational ideas, demanding that the governments of America or Great Britain send divers down to rescue those who might have survived and remained trapped within the ship's walls. Others demanded that the ship itself be raised, a plan that was far from feasible but remained popular for decades. Besides the depth to which the ship sank, more than 12,000 feet down, any plans for finding the ship were severely hampered by the fact that, given that she continued to drift even after hitting the iceberg, no one knew where she had ended up. Even the iceberg that brought her down continued to drift slowly from its destination. This left an area of at least 3,600 square miles through which anyone hoping to locate the fallen ship would have to look, and though there were many who would happily have backed a recovery effort, it soon became clear that, with the technology available in 1912, no such effort could ever succeed.

Investigation, Blame and Prevention

New York newspaper headlines about the *Titanic*

The *Carpathia* in New York with the survivors of the *Titanic* aboard

"About 6.30 a. m. we got an unofficial message from the Carpathia to the Baltic: The Titanic has gone down with all hands, as far as we know, with the exception of 20 boatloads, which we have picked up. Number not accurately fixed yet. We cannot see any more boats about at all. That was just sent from the operator of the Carpathia to the captain of the Baltic. That went to Captain Ranson.

In reply, the captain sent that message: Can I be of any assistance to you as regards taking some of the passengers from you? Will be in the position about 4.30. Let me know if you alter your position.

COMMANDER BALTIC.

At 7.10 we received a message from the Carpathia, from the captain of the Carpathia to the captain of the Baltic. 'Am proceeding for Halifax or New York, full speed .You had better proceed to Liverpool. Have about 800 passengers aboard.'" - Gilbert Balfour, Marconi Co., Inspector on the *Baltic*

Without any hope of bringing the *Titanic*, or any more of her victims home, the countries most closely involved with her loss began to plan investigations into what went wrong. Senator

William A. Smith, a Michigan Republican, contacted the White House and asked that President Taft launch some sort of investigation. When Taft refused, Smith took his concerns to the United States Senate and convinced his colleagues to appoint a committee to investigate the disaster. He also volunteered to chair that committee and to handpick its members. He went on to choose Jonathan Bourne, an Oregon Republican who had once been shipwrecked off the coast of Asia. He then added Theodore Burton, the Republican chairman of the National Waterways Commission, and Duncan Fletcher, a Florida Democrat who represented a number of titans of industry. Francis G. Newlands, a Democrat from Nevada, George Perkins, a California Republican who had been at sea as a boy and Furnifold Simmons, a Democrat from North Carolina rounded out the committee.

While the Americans were organizing their committee, the British government was also establishing a Board of Inquiry, with Charles Bigham, Lord Mersey of Toxeth at its head. Some would later accuse Mersey of covering up mistakes made by the Board of Trade but the transcripts themselves paint a picture of a man determinedly looking for the truth. He was joined in his efforts by J. Harvard Biles, Professor of Naval Architecture at the University of Glasgow and Rear Admiral S. A. Gough-Calthorpe of the Royal Navy, as well as Edward C. Chaston, who was probably brought on board the committee to lend his technical expertise to the proceedings, Captain A.W. Clarke, a Master of the Admiralty Court and Commander F. C. A. Lyon, formerly of the Royal Navy.

The first and most important question that both committees had to try to answer was why the *Titanic* ran into the iceberg at all. John Simon, the solicitor general for the British Board of Trade, questioned George Turnbull, the Deputy-Manager for the Marconi International Marine Communication Company, about when and how many warnings the ship had received about icebergs in the area. He determined that there was at least one message sent but that it may have been misplaced. Smith himself questioned Harold Bride, the only telegrapher to survive the wreck about this.

Following on the heels of questions about the messages the ship received or lack thereof came questions about how fast the *Titanic* was going in the moments leading up to the tragedy. When questioned, Ismay maintained that he never saw the ship go unusually fast. Simon questioned Charles Lightoller, the ship's navigator, about his opinion but found him difficult to pin down, primarily because there are no posted speed limits on the high seas.

Meanwhile, Smith focused most of his line of questioning on the state of the watertight compartments. When questioning another navigator, Herman J. Pittman, he learned that it was unclear whether or not all the compartments were appropriately closed and sealed. At the same time, Pittman reminded the committee that, because of the way in which the ship was constructed, it was unlikely that closing all the compartments would have made that much difference. The British board in turn addressed this issue during its investigation.

Since the day she went down, much has been made of the idea that most of the passengers lost had been housed in steerage. Senator Smith questioned Daniel Buckley, himself a passenger in Third Class, about any gates or doors that might have kept those in steerage from escaping safely. What came out was that any gate that was locked was easily broken through when the situation reached a crisis level and so no one was left to drown. Thus it seems that the reason that so many in the lower decks lost their lives was simply that they were too far away from the crash to learn what was going on in time to safely board a lifeboat.

Without a doubt, the most hated witness present at the hearings was Bruce Ismay. Many were furious that the Managing Director of the White Star Line had saved his own skin when so many other men nobly perished. Ismay knew he was in trouble and planned to sail back to England without ever landing on American soil. However, the Senate got wind of this plot and subpoenaed him, forcing him to appear before it on April 18. Throughout his questioning, Ismay managed to avoid admitting that he was one of the men behind eliminating some of the lifeboats.

While the outcome no doubt would have been different if *Titanic* had had a full complement of lifeboats, the biggest problem addressed by the investigating committee in America concerned how chaotic and disorganized things were on deck the night the ship sank. These questions in turn evolved into an investigation of what types of distress signals were sent out and who received them. The *Frankfurt* was heartily criticized for ignoring the vessel's pleas for help while those aboard the *Carpathia* were praised. Captain Stanley Lord of the *Californian* was also censured for not responding quickly to *Titanic*'s flare signals, which members of its crew admitted seeing.

While hearings were being held on both sides of the Atlantic, the Case of the Lost Ship was also being tried in the papers. As was mentioned before, Yellow Journalism, with all the sensationalism and half-truths that goes with it was alive and well in 1912 and newspaper men tracked down one survivor after another to get his or her story. The *Titanic* was hot news and many were determined to make a buck or two off the tragedy.

Ultimately, the two committees finished that work and published their findings for the general public. The British Committee was most concerned with the facts of the matter and what could be learned from the incident, concluding that the ship's "excessive speed" was primarily to blame for the accident. It also headed criticism on the *Californian* but exonerated Captain Smith, saying that he only did what any other man in his position would have done. Finally, they even cleared the White Star Line from any responsibility for what happened.

A picture of *Titanic* passenger Sir Cosmo Duff Gordon testifying before the British inquiry

Because they had no authority to make substantive changes to the way things were being done, the Senate Committee focused most of its energy on making recommendations for stricter and wider reaching, seafaring codes. The committee heaped its most aggressive criticism on the White Star Line and anyone else who was involved with the ship's design or construction. It was particularly critical of the way in which those in charge of getting the passengers onto the lifeboats had, or more precisely had not, been trained. It even criticized the late Captain Smith and the British Committee itself. The British Committee responded in kind, insisting that Smith and the other committee members lacked the seafaring experience needed to pass judgment on the case.

It was left to Senator Isidor Rayner to conclude the hearings by saying:

"As the ship was sinking, the strains of music were wafting over the deck. ... It was a rallying cry for the living and the dying - to rally them not for life, but to rally them for their awaiting death. Almost face to face with their Creator, amid the chaos of this supreme and solemn moment, in inspiring notes the unison resounded through the ship. It told the victims of the wreck that there was another world beyond the seas, free from the agony of pain, and, though with somber tones, it cheered them on to their untimely fate. As the sea closed upon the heroic dead, let us feel that the heavens opened to the lives that were prepared to enter.

"…If the melody that was rehearsed could only reverberate through this land 'Nearer, My God, to Thee,' and its echoes could be heard in these halls of legislation, and at every place where our rulers and representatives pass judgment and enact and administer laws, and at every home and fireside…and if we could be made to feel that there is a divine law of obedience and of adjustment…far above the laws that we formulate in this presence, then, from the gloom of these fearful hours we shall pass into the dawn of a higher service and of a better day, and then…the lives that went down upon this fated night did not go down in vain."

Not satisfied to simply criticize, the American committee demanded that changes be made to international regulations governing the number of lifeboats a ship be required to carry, as well as how crewmen should be trained to man them. These changes were implemented by the International Convention for the Safety of Life at Sea in 1914, which also changed the rules concerning how distress signals were used at sea, insisting the red flares always be seen as a call for help. Meanwhile, the British Committee did insist that in the future ships should be built with higher bulkheads so that their watertight compartments would indeed be watertight. Most significant of all, however, was the creation of the International Ice Patrol, which still works hand in hand with the U.S. Coast Guard to watch for ice in the North Atlantic and warn ships of its location. Every April 15, the Patrol lays a wreath at the site of *Titanic*'s watery grave.

A cartoon calling for regulations in the wake of the disaster

Lost and Found

"When I first set out after the Titanic, it was sort of a mechanical, technical problem. My soul was not in it. My mind was in it. But in the course of getting ready, I had to study it and I met a man by the name of Bill Tantum who died just before I found the Titanic. Bill was the soul of the Titanic. He lived in Connecticut, and he started the Titanic Historical Society. He had been injured in Korea, always wanted to be career Army officer, but he got hurt. His dream went away, and he needed a new dream, and it became the Titanic. This man lived and breathed Captain Smith. When you sat and talked with him, you talked with the past. He knew how many buttons the Captain had on his uniform. He knew everything about it. I was going after him in a very investigative reporter way, but in the course of asking those questions, I had to listen to all this other stuff. It enters your soul, that tragedy. I wasn't terribly conscious of that, until I found it. Then it blew me right over, like a truck ran over the top of me. It was months before I could deal with it emotionally. It was a complete surprise." - Robert Ballard

As was mentioned before, people have been fascinated with locating the *Titanic* since it went down in 1912. In fact, more might have been done sooner to find the lost ship had World War I not intervened. Indeed, it took another World War to begin developing the kind of technology that would ultimately be used to locate the wreck, specifically sonar, which can locate underwater objects by bouncing off sound waves off of them and measuring how they return. The end of World War II also brought about a new level of prosperity that allowed men like Risdon Beazley to raise money to look for the ship. In July 1953, he began setting off depth charges near the *Titanic's* last known location and recording the waves they gave off with sonar. However, he never found the ship.

Nor did Douglas Wooley, who began seriously looking in 1966. Believing that the ship had sunk in one piece, he believed he could raise it if he found it. Using £40,000 he obtained from investors, he teamed up with two Hungarian scientists and took a boat loaded with what was then state of the art sonar equipment and underwater cameras. He intended to explore the area and then send down a bathyscaphe (a deep sea submarine connected to the ocean's surface by a float). He hoped to then raise the ship with a bunch of nylon balloons. However, he ran into problems when his investors learned that that portion of the project alone would take more than ten years.

While everyone from respected scientists to crackpots were discussing whether or not it could ever be raised, a young man named Robert Ballard was growing up reading *20,000 Leagues Under the Sea*. He went on to become an oceanographer and get a job at the Woods Hole Oceanographic Institution. He also began to wonder if he could find the *Titanic*. After years of research, he found enough investors to join him to form Seasonics International Limited, a company whose main purpose was to find the *Titanic*. He made his first trip in search of the vessel in 1977, using a rented drillship designed for salvaging wrecks. Not only did he return home without finding the *Titanic*, he also came back without $600,000 of gear that he lost when its remote-controlled claw broke.

Ballard

  While Ballard backed off to regroup, millionaire Jack Grimm launched a search for the ship in July, 1980. His mission also failed to find the ship, though he later learned that he had sailed over the wreck without knowing it was there. Grimm returned to the area in 1981 and again in 1983 but never found the ship. He might have continued his futile attempts had Ballard not returned to the scene, both figuratively and literally.

  In the five years since his first failed attempt to find the ship, Ballard had worked with the United States Navy to develop a robotic submarine that he hoped to one day use to find the *Titanic*. Himself a Navy veteran, Ballard convinced the Deputy Chief of Naval Operations for Submarine Warfare, N. Ronald Thunman, that such a device could help the Navy find the *U.S.S. Thresher* and the *U.S.S. Scorpion*, two submarines that had gone down in the same part of the ocean as *Titanic*. Ballard already had plans for a submersible he called Argo that could dive as deep as 20,000 feet. It had no engine and would carry no passengers, leaving more space for cameras and equipment. Instead, it would be towed along the bottom of the ocean by some surface vessel. After much negotiation, the Navy agreed to pay for a mission to find its lost submarines and that, once he accomplished that, Ballard could use whatever time he had left in the area to search for *Titanic*.

Ballard left for the North Atlantic in June 1985 and quickly found the two missing subs. During his work for the Navy, he also learned that a sinking ship leaves behind a debris field that can extend for quite some distance. He reasoned that such a trail would be present at the sight of the *Titanic*, too. Using this information, he stopped depending on SONAR to look for just the ship and started using cameras to search for smaller items that would lead him to the ship.

Ballard's efforts paid off and after just two weeks of consistent searching, he located the first debris from *Titanic* on September 1, 1985. After initially celebrating with clapping and shouts of joy, the men suddenly realized just what they were seeing, the final resting place of hundreds of people who had lost their lives there. At that point their laughter gave way to a more somber and respectful celebration that what was once lost had been found, though those dead could never be brought back to life.

Ballard would later admit that looking at the debris field was emotionally draining, as stacks of still intact china sat beside chairs where beautiful young women had once sat and beds children had slept in. He later recalled finding a case of still corked wine and red and white tiles that once decorated a wall. However, the most emotional objects for him were the shoes, for their tough leather had survived where nothing else had, not even the feet that had been wearing them when they settled on the bottom of the ocean. He soon realized that every pair of shoes lying side by side represented a life snuffed out and a body long ago taken by the sea.

A picture of the remains of Captain Smith's personal bathroom

A pocket watch permanently frozen at 2:28, minutes after the *Titanic* sank

A picture of a decaying piece of the ship

Like the trail of bread crumbs in Hansel and Gretel, the debris trail soon led Ballard and his crew to their prize. He later explained that when the ship landed, it hit so hard that it sunk 60 feet down into the ocean's floor. As they maneuvered Argo up its side, they saw rows and rows of portholes, looking back at them, Ballard later said, like the eyes of the dead. No doubt the team would have remained for weeks at the spot but the weather was turning bad and the Navy wanted its equipment back, so they soon returned to the United States, where they were greeted with a hero's welcome.

Having finally found the ship, Ballard soon found himself inundated with offers to back its exploration. This new infusion of funds allowed him to develop Alvin, a small deep sea submarine that could take three people to the depths of the ocean, two and a half miles below the surface, to explore the wreck. In addition to human passengers, Alvin also carried Jason, Jr., aka JJ, a small remote control robot that could actually be sent inside the ship to send back real time video of what it "saw."

In June, 1986, the Atlantis II returned to the sight of the wreck and Ballard dove for the first time in Alvin. After a few tense moments when equipment malfunctioned and had to be adjusted, the men arrived at the keel of *Titanic* itself, the first human beings to be that close to the ship in 75 years. They quickly determined that the ship indeed had broken apart when it sank, leaving the two halves about a third of a mile apart. When it hit the ocean floor, the stern had collapsed, causing all the decks to pancake down on each other on the bottom of the ocean.

The team continued to work out the kinks in the project over the next several days, finally mastering both the equipment and the site itself. On the third day of diving, they were able to sail comfortably around the ship, basking in the pleasure of all they were seeing. One of their biggest thrills was to be able to send JJ into the ship proper, into spaces too small for Alvin to ever go. The men later described the strange sensation of what they were seeing as making them feel somehow out of scale, at some moments tiny, at others gigantic.

Unfortunately, Alvin could not hold enough oxygen to allow the men to remain down for long, leisurely trips. Instead, they had to move quickly from space to space, constantly making sure to make the best use of their time. As a result the trips, while thrilling, were far from comfortable. Still, they persevered on, determined to find the one Holy Grail they were looking for, the sight of the ship's name emblazoned on its hull. This prize, unfortunately, eluded them. Instead, they had to leave the area once again, this time leaving behind a memorial plaque commemorating their discovery and honoring the lives of those who rested at the bottom of the sea.

Following the Money to Oblivion?

"RMS Titanic, Inc. was formed for the purpose of exploring the wreck of Titanic and its surrounding ocean areas; obtaining oceanographic material and scientific data; and using the data and retrieved artifacts for historical verification, scientific education and public awareness. Serving as the exclusive salvor in possession of the wreck site, RMS Titanic, Inc. is committed to engaging the global community in Titanic's story through educational, historical, scientific and conservation based programs." - *RMS Titanic*, Inc. website

When Ballard left the *Titanic* in 1986, it was with a new understanding and appreciation for what the site really was, a mass grave. As a result, he abandoned his original plans to salvage items from the wreck and instead focused his attention on preserving it intact, supporting the *RMS Titanic* Maritime Memorial Act passed by the United States Congress on October 21, 1986. In addition to formally defining *Titanic* as a historical artifact, the act encouraged international dialogue about how it could best be protected. Since the *Titanic* lay in international waters, no country had the authority on its own to protect the remains and many countries were unconcerned about what happened to the ship.

In 1987, the French Research Institute for Exploitation of the Sea, which had joined Ballard in the 1985 dive, contracted with *Titanic* Ventures to explore the site and bring back as many objects as possible from the ocean floor. Over the course of twenty-three dives, the company recovered more than 1,800 artifacts from the ship, including the bell that rang on April 14, 1912 when the iceberg was spotted.

Four years later, in 1991, underwater explorers from Russia, Canada and the United States used two MIR submersibles to carry twenty men down to the site seventeen times. Representatives of CBS, National Geographic, and IMAX shot more than 100 hours of film that later became *Titanica*, a documentary completed in IMAX in 1995. In 1993, *Titanic* Ventures became *RMS Titanic*, Inc. (RMST). It sponsored another expedition, this time bringing back more than 800 items from the wreck, including a two ton reciprocating engine. It also established itself in maritime court as salver-in-possession of the site in 1994, meaning that it could claim exclusive rights to salvage the area as long as it made at least one dive every two years. RMST's 1994 expedition brought up more than 1,000 objects and this led to the opening of the *Titanic* exhibit at the National Maritime Museum in Greenwich, England in October of that year. This renewed interest in the wreck and this led to an agreement among the United Kingdom, France, Canada and the United States to regulate salvage efforts at the site.

Meanwhile, a new wrinkle developed in the *Titanic* situation. The Liverpool and London Steamship Protection and Indemnity Association, who had initially insured many of *Titanic*'s wealthier passengers and thus had paid claims to people who had lost property in the wreck, demanded that it receive either some of the property it had paid for eighty years earlier or some of the profits from its sale.

Always looking for a new way to cash in on what it controlled, RMST offered a cruise ship the opportunity to visit the site in 1996. Passengers aboard could sail in comfort on the surface while watching divers work at the bottom of the ocean. The experience proved to be something of a disappointment for all concerned and the cruise company later sued RMST for $8 million. The following year, the Discovery Channel broadcast *Titanic: Anatomy of a Disaster*, featuring footage from this expedition.

Meanwhile, in 1996 James Cameron began work on what would become the most famous film yet made about the doomed ship. After visiting the site himself in a submersible, he recreated what he saw for the film's opening scenes. *Titanic* opened in 1997 to a fanfare of enthusiasm. Though many have since panned the film, it nonetheless brought the ship once more into the public spotlight and led in 1999 to the "Operation *Titanic*" venture, launched by Deep Ocean Expeditions.

For the first time in history, anyone willing to pay $32,500 could travel in a Russian submarine two and a half miles down to see the wreck itself. For their money, those waiting their turn for the ultimate tourist experience could reside in comfort on the waters above. Despite RMST's legal objections, this proved to be the first of many such trips that would be made to the site.

Now that it could no longer claim exclusive rights to photograph the ship's remains, RMST stepped up its salvage efforts and announced in 2000 that it would be focusing its attention on "high profile targets," including a diamond shipment that was said to be worth upwards of $300 million. This only fueled accusations that the company was only out to make a buck and led those in charge to hire an archaeologist who was supposed to create a historical context for the pieces being salvaged.

By this time, the courts had had enough of RMST and its questionable activities. In July 2000, a district judge forbade the company to in any way damage or alter the ship during its treasure hunting activities. It also ruled that it could not sell anything it brought up for profit. This meant that the only way that RMST could recoup its investment was to put the items on display and charge patrons to see them.

By this time, the United States, Great Britain, Canada and France finally completed a joint resolution recognizing *Titanic* as a gravesite and laying down rules for how it should be treated. Their efforts were widely praised, especially by the National Oceanic and Atmospheric Administration. However, their plan was far from perfect, for there was no way in which they could consistently police the area to enforce their will. Still, it was a beginning and that mattered, especially to Robert Ballard who, over the years, came to regret very much his role in finding the ship and exposing its remains to the world. He was even more disturbed when he returned to the wreck in 2004 and saw the damage that had been done by the submersibles that came after his.

Of course, there have been some good, even noble ventures to the wreck, such as the one that took Philip Littlejohn, whose grandfather had been a crew member, down. He, like others, found the trip unforgettable. Still, as more tourists are allowed down, the submarines taking them will likely become larger and therefore more damaging to the ship and the area around it. Inspired by James Cameron's 2001 3-D work for Disney, *Ghosts of the Abyss*, Ballard teamed up with the National Oceanic and Atmospheric Administration on their 2003 and 2004 trips down to assess the *Titanic*'s current and future stability. His plan is to use that footage to record the ship's look in so much detail that a 3-D documentary could be created that would allow viewers to get a sense of the ship's grandeur without visiting it in person. He later added a plan to place bright underwater lights and video cameras around the wreck. These in turn would live stream video of the ocean floor to computers all over the world.

But there was another purpose behind this trip, and that was to get footage that might someday be all that is left of the ship, for even without the damage inflicted by human visitors, the *Titanic* is slowly decaying in its watery grave. In 2005, James Cameron visited the *Titanic* to film *Last Mysteries of the Titanic*, admitting that he did not believe the ship would last much longer. Ballard, however, remains optimistic about the sea's effect on the ship but pessimistic about what man is doing to it.

And perhaps he has good reason for this because anxious to get what it could while it could, Premier Exhibitions, Inc., a part of RMST, in 2007 bought the rights of all the personal belongings found on the ship. In 2011, U.S. District Judge Rebecca Beach Smith ruled that the company had the right to the items, as long as they properly cared for and preserved them. While this has allowed new *Titanic* museums and tourists attractions to spring up around the world, it also means that the ship will continue to be plundered. In the end, it seems that whether nature wipes it out or men plunder it into oblivion, *Titanic*'s days remain just as numbered as they were on that fateful April day on which she was launched.

The Lusitania

The Largest Ship in the World

The *Lusitania* before it was launched

"The ship was built of steel by John Brown and Company, at Clydebank, in 1907. She had a length of 769.33 feet and a breadth of 87.85, with a depth of 61.72. She was fore and aft rigged; she was fitted with six steam turbine engines of 65,000 indicated horse power, equal to a speed of 24 knots-that is, when all the boilers were working. She was registered at Liverpool, and her tonnage after deducting 17,784 tons for propelling power and crew space was 12,611. The ship was built under the special survey of the Admiralty and the Admiralty requirements. She had accommodation including the crew for over 3,000 persons." - Sir Edward Carson, a Member of Parliament and the King's Council, at the opening of the investigation into the loss of the *Lusitania*.

The *Lusitania* will forever be remembered as a result of the way in which it sank, but it's important to remember that the ship was, in many ways, a hybrid. For instance, the ship was built by a company named Cunard to be used as a passenger liner, much like the *Queen Mary* and the *Olympic* were. Cunard consisted of a group of investors who put a lot of money into the ship's construction in order to make it back, preferably with a profit, but the company also had a secret partner when they built the *Lusitania*. The ship's construction was supplemented by the government of Great Britain, with the understanding that should a war ever break out, the ship would be used by the government as an Armed Merchant Cruiser.

A picture with the *Olympic* in the front and the *Lusitania* in the background

According to Alexander Galbraith, a Superintending Engineer to the Cunard Line, the *Lusitania* was built to the highest specifications of the day: "The vessel was built throughout of steel and had a cellular double bottom of the usual type, with a floor at every frame, its depth at the center line being 60 inches, except in the way of turbine machinery, where it was 72 inches.

This double bottom extended up the ship's side to a height of 8 feet above the keel. Above the double bottom the vessel was constructed on the usual transverse frame system, reinforced by web frames, which extended to the highest decks. At the forward end the framing and plating was strengthened with a view to preventing panting, and damage when meeting ice. Beams were fitted on every frame at all decks from the boat deck downwards. An external bilge keel about 300 feet long and 30 inches deep was fitted along the bilge amidships. The heavy plating was carried up to the shelter deck. Between the shelter deck and below the upper deck a depth of 14 feet 6 inches was double plated and hydraulic riveted. The stringer plate of the shelter deck was also doubled. All decks were steel plated throughout, The transverse strength of the ship was in part dependent on the 12 transverse watertight bulkheads which were specially strengthened and stiffened to enable them to stand the necessary pressure in the event of accident, and they were connected by double angles to decks, inner bottom and shell plating."

Likewise, the ship was powered by a state-of-the-art engine that was designed to allow the ship to move at speeds up to 28 knots (over 32 miles per hour), considered quite fast at the time. In fact, the *Lusitania*'s maximum speed, and what it took to make the ship move at top speed, would later be a major issue in the investigation surrounding the sinking. Galbraith added, "The main propelling machinery consisted of two high pressure ahead turbines, two low pressure ahead, and two astern turbines, driving four lines of main shafting. The two outer lines of shafting were each driven by a high pressure ahead turbine. The two inner lines of shafting were each driven by a low pressure ahead turbine. Forward of each low pressure ahead turbine and on the same line of shafting was an astern turbine, so that when going astern only the inner shafts were driving the ship. Steam was supplied by 23 double ended boilers and two single ended boilers, arranged for a working pressure of 195 lbs. per square inch."

The *Lusitania* before its launch

A picture of the *Lusitania's* First Class Drawing Room

A picture of the *Lusitania's* First Class Dining Room

Though the ship was built five years before the Titanic, the *Lusitania* had been the beneficiary of many improvements demanded by travelers following the *Titanic's* scandalous loss. As Sir Edward Carson pointed out, "She was fitted with 15 transverse bulkheads. The longest compartment was the forward boiler room, which was over 90 feet long, and all the watertight doors and the bulkheads could by special arrangements he closed simultaneously; and I think there is evidence that that was done on this occasion." The *Lusitania* also had what many felt would be enough to keep her afloat, a "double bottom, the depth between the outer and the inner being 5 feet at the center."

When the *Lusitania* made its maiden voyage, it surpassed everyone's expectations, and on its second voyage, it set the record for quickest transatlantic voyage by making finishing the trip in less than 5 days. Though the ship would not hold the record for long, its successes quickly made it a favorite on both sides of the Atlantic.

The Lusitania on its maiden voyage

The Lusitania sailing past Battery Park, New York City on its maiden trip

The Lusitania docking in *New York City* for the first time

A 1910 postcard featuring the *Lusitania* in New York City

The Start of World War I

A picture of mail being delivered off the *Lusitania*

"She had aboard 4,200 cases of cartridges, but they were cartridges for small arms, packed in separate cases... they certainly do not come under the classification of ammunition. The United States authorities would not permit us to carry ammunition, classified as such by the military authorities, on a passenger liner. For years we have been sending small-arms cartridges abroad on the Lusitania." – Herman Winter, Assistant Manager of the Cunard Line, May 10, 1915

With the outbreak of World War I, the *Lusitania* was officially designated an Armed Merchant Cruiser, but at the same time, the ship continued to ply the waters as a civilian ocean liner, supposedly under the protection of the Cruiser Rules, a set of rules developed during the latter half of the 19th century to cover how civilian vessels would be treated during a time of war. The rules allowed for navies to capture an enemy's civilian ships, but if they did so, they had to provide safe passage for the non-military passengers on board. In the same vein, it forbade the targeting of civilian vessels by military ships.

The *Lusitania* continued to cross the Atlantic, a journey it made over 200 times by the middle of April 1915. Nonetheless, travel during wartime is always dangerous, and by then, everyone was nervous about what was going on in the Atlantic, primarily because of the newly designed German submarines that were patrolling the waters. The Germans were trying to prevent ships from reaching the coasts of the United Kingdom and let noncombatants know the zones in which their navies were operating.

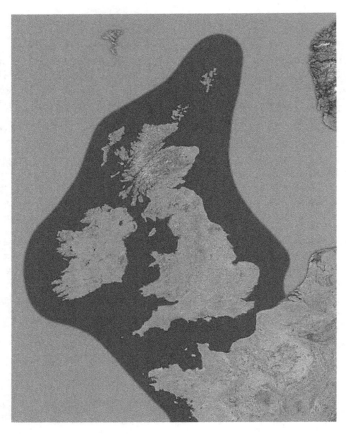

A map of the exclusion zone, a zone in which Germany claimed the right to attack or seize and search ships

At the urging of a number of concerned Americans of German heritage, the German Embassy in the United States went so far as to publish the following warning just days before the *Lusitania* left New York on what would be her final voyage:

> "NOTICE! TRAVELLERS intending to embark on the Atlantic voyage are reminded that a state of war exists between Germany and her allies and Great Britain and her allies; that the zone of war includes the waters adjacent to the British Isles; that, in accordance with formal notice given by the Imperial German Government, vessels flying the flag of Great Britain, or any of her allies, are liable

to destruction in those waters and that travelers sailing in the war zone on the ships of Great Britain or her allies do so at their own risk.
IMPERIAL GERMAN EMBASSY
Washington, D.C., April 22, 1915"

The German Embassy's warning was printed alongside an advertisement for the *Lusitania*'s voyage

Woodrow Wilson's administration knew the Germans' U-boat policy and was already warning Germany not to target civilian ships, and on May 1, the very day that passengers were boarding the *Lusitania* on its trip back across the Atlantic, the president told Americans that "no warning that an unlawful and inhumane act will be committed" could justify actually conducting the attack. However, while many who boarded the *Lusitania* on May 1, 1915 had seen the German embassy's warning, most chose to disregard it, some for rather unusual reasons. For example, some believed that if the trip was truly dangerous, a warning would have been issued from a more reliable source than the Germans. Theodore Naish, traveling in Second Class with his wife, Belle, told her, "We will not worry. No reputable newspaper would accept an advertisement of that Cunard Line size and in it put another in direct opposition. It would be like advertising 'John Taylor Dry Goods Kansas City Missouri' and then inserting 'The Peck Dry Goods Company warns patrons of John Taylor Company as said goods are worthless or stolen.' If that were official, the notice would have been posted in glaring signs, and each American passenger would have had warning sent and delivered before boarding the vessel."

Others weren't about to let the danger or warnings scare them off. Phoebe Amory later admitted, "[I]t is only natural, and not to be attributed to a desire to boast, that I should have made the voyage warning or no warning."

Of course, many passengers understandably found the German warning worrisome, including Reverend Clark, who later recalled the trepidation he experienced even as he was booking his passage on the ship: "I only asked the man who gave me my ticket whether there was any extraordinary danger in travelling by the *Lusitania* and he told me, no, there was none as far as he knew, and that the Cunard Company were not likely to risk a ship of such enormous value if there was any extra danger. [Staff Captain James Clarke Anderson] told me almost at the beginning of the voyage that six of the boilers had been cut off and that the result of that was that 1000 tons of coal would be saved on the voyage and I asked him a question or two…I asked him if that was altogether giving us the best chance, and his answer was that as the Germans had not succeeded in torpedoing any vessel that was going more than 12 knots an hour, and as the *Lusitania* with the boilers which were in commission could comfortably go 21 or 22 knots, it was considered that there was an ample margin of safety."

The changes Reverend Clark was referencing were made in response to the outbreak of the war and the shortages in both fuel and manpower that the fighting had brought. Not only were many young men who might otherwise have fired engines on civilian crafts joining the Navy, the coal used in luxury liners was also needed for naval ships. Alfred Allen Booth, Chairman of the Cunard Line, later explained, "That change was made, not at the outbreak of the war, but in November, I think. After the rush of homeward - bound American traffic was over, and that came to an end towards the end of October, it became a question as to whether we could continue running the two large steamers the *Lusitania* and the 'Mauretania' at all or not. We went into the matter very carefully and we came to the conclusion that it would be possible to continue running one of them at a reduced speed, that is to say, that the traffic would be sufficient, but only sufficient to justify running one steamer a month if we reduced the expense. To run it to pay expenses. We did not hope to make any profit, and as a matter of fact we did not make any profit. We decided to run the *Lusitania*, not the 'Mauretania,' at ¾ - boiler power, and that meant a reduction of speed from an average of about 24 knots to an average of about 21 knots. It would result in a considerable reduction in the total consumption of coal, and also a reduction in the number of men required for the crew, both of which were important."

The *Mauretania* and *Lusitania*

While the changes did result in savings, passengers such as Clark were worried that they might also make the *Lusitania* a sitting duck for the German submarines. Booth later had to answer these allegations, as well as explain the measures he and the other leaders of the Cunard Line took to respond to the published German threat. He explained, "I do not think I heard anything about the special threats made in New York until the Sunday morning after she had sailed. I have been trying to remember whether I heard on the Saturday. I cannot remember whether I did, but I understand the threats were published in New York on the Saturday morning. Therefore, I do not think I could have heard until the Saturday evening at the earliest. I certainly remember knowing it on the Sunday but not on the Saturday. I should not generally put a subject of that kind down for specific discussion at a Board Meeting or a Committee Meeting of Directors. I am in constant touch with them every day and with my Managers, and I have no recollection now of any specific discussion on that point, I am quite sure if there had been we should have felt that we could not make any difference in our action. It was a question of either running the *Lusitania* at 21 knots or not running her at all; and I know my own view would have been strongly against withdrawing the ship entirely on the submarine threat, and I think that I must in conversation with my Directors have learned that that was also their view. Certainly, it was taken for granted as far as I am concerned."

In Booth's mind, the most important thing was that the captains of the individual ships in the line be made aware of what was going on. He felt that they would then be the best judges about how to proceed based on their years of experience and training: "We discussed the submarine danger with the individual captains - either I or my immediate assistant in every case, but the discussion had necessarily to be of the nature of making sure that they realized what the general dangers were. We could not venture to give specific instructions when in an emergency they would be in possession of facts which could not be in our possession, and we felt it would be very dangerous to attempt to give specific instructions when the circumstances might make those instructions absolutely dangerous to follow. … We discussed the general form the danger would take and the general methods whereby it could best be avoided. One of the particular points of course was the question of closing the watertight doors when in the danger zone, swinging out the boats, seeing that all the ports were closed, seeing that everything was ready in the boats; and another point was the danger of stopping in the danger zone to pick up a pilot or stopping at the Liverpool Bar to wait for the tide to rise."

Tragically, the dangers would soon be realized.

Bound for Liverpool

A 1908 photo of the *Lusitania* headed for Liverpool

"*The steamship Lusitania which was both a passenger ship and an emigrant ship … belonging to the Cunard Line, was, at the end of April, at New York, and was about to sail for England on the first of May. She left New York about noon on the 1st of May with a crew, …a large number of passengers, and a general cargo, bound for Liverpool…On the morning of the 6th May…all the Class A lifeboats, amounting to 22, were swung outwards under the superintendence of the proper officer and were left swinging and ready for lowering.*" - Sir Edward Carson

Early in the morning of May 1, 1915, more than 600 blurry-eyed seamen made their way onto the *Lusitania* to prepare the ship for departure. All but 25 of them were men, and they were mostly young adults who had signed up for a life at sea in the hopes of seeing the world and having a few adventures. In fact, many of them had been up drinking late into the night and were now trying to sober up enough to do their jobs. They joined those who had stood watch through the night to make up the ship's full complement of 702. About 300 reported to the ship's engine rooms to prepare for launch later that day, while another 300 busied themselves checking staterooms and dining saloons to make sure all was in readiness for the passenger's comfort. The rest scattered throughout the ship to do their assigned tasks.

A few hours after the last crewman was aboard, the passengers started to board. As was the practice at the time, the Third Class (steerage) passengers made their way to their cabins through their own entrance, separate from the entrance set aside for the First and Second Class passengers. About 600 men, women and children headed to steerage, and the other 660 passengers boarding the ship were divided pretty evenly between First Class and steerage. The ship itself was well-designed and cared for, with much thought having been given to the passengers' comfort. Theodore Diamandis, a steerage passenger from Greece, later mentioned, "There is not any promenade deck in the third class on the port side. It is an entrance to the second class. ... That deck is a long deck for the third class passengers to promenade and the other is for the second class passengers. That is the long deck - the promenade deck."

Following the loss of the *Titanic* three years earlier, there had been an increase in both the number of lifeboat drills required for an ocean liner and in the passengers' interest in them. Reverend Clark observed a drill not long after he boarded the ship: "At 11 o'clock there was a bell rung and there was a boat which was kept swung out all the time during the voyage as far as I know, and a number of men came and got into the boat, put on lifebelts for a few seconds and took them off again, the boat not being moved all this time; then they jumped out of the boat and ran back." While strides had definitely been made since the sinking of the *Titanic*, which took 3 hours to sink after striking an iceberg, the additional lifeboat drills would prove to be insufficient preparation for a torpedoed ship that sank in less than 20 minutes.

A picture of passengers and collapsible lifeboats on the *Lusitania*

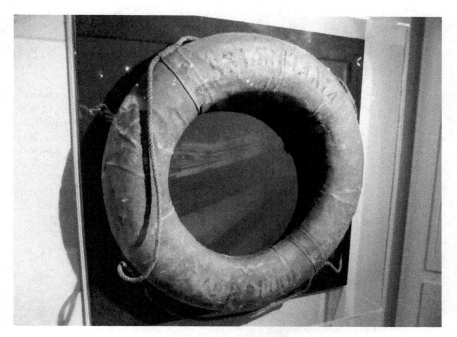

One of the *Lusitania*'s lifebelts

For the most part, the voyage was uneventful, but as the *Lusitania* approached the English coast, the ship's captain and crew became more cautious. The shore near Liverpool was considered particularly dangerous because so many submarines had been spotted in the area. In describing the recommendations Cunard had given her captains, Booth said, "It was one of the points that we felt it necessary to make the Captain of the *Lusitania* understand the importance of. The *Lusitania* can only cross the Liverpool Bar at certain states of the tide, and we therefore warned the captain, or whoever might be captain, that we did not think it would be safe for him to arrive off the bar at such a time that he would have to wait there, because that area had been infested with submarines, and we thought therefore it would be wiser for him to arrange his arrival in such a way, leaving him an absolutely free hand as to how he would do it, that he could come straight up without stopping at all. The one definite instruction we did give him with regard to that was to authorize him to come up without a pilot."

On the morning of May 7, passengers who paid attention to such things would have noticed that the lifeboats had been uncovered and swung out to the sides of the ship. If any took the time to ask a crewman why this had been done, they might not have liked the answer. Sir Edward Carson explained, "That was in consequence of the ship then approaching what may be called the war zone or the danger zone. About 10 minutes past 2 p.m. on the 7th May the vessel was off the Irish Coast. She had passed early in the morning the Fastnet Rock at the extreme corner where you turn round to come up the Irish Channel, and had arrived at 2.10 near the Old Head of Kinsale. …The ship was about 8 to 10 miles off the Old Head of Kinsale. One of the questions which will arise on the evidence is as to whether that was, at the time and under the circumstances which your Lordship will hear, a proper place for the captain to be navigating. The weather was fine and clear and the sea was smooth and the vessel was making about 18 knots." The passengers could not have known it, but all the watertight bulkheads located in the lower parts of the ship had also been closed and sealed. Ironically, the fact that the watertight compartments were closed ahead of time meant some crewmen would be trapped in them when the ship was torpedoed and thus had no chance to escape the sinking ship.

One of the things that came out during the investigation of the loss of the *Lusitania* was that, considering the dangerous water in which he found himself, Captain William Thomas Turner was charting a rather relaxed course, as indicated by the conversation between him and Clem Edwards, a representative of the seamen's union:

> "Edwards: At the time you were struck were you steering a perfectly straight course?
> Turner: As straight as you can steer.
>
> Edwards: To get that maximum speed how many of the boilers had to be fired?
> Turner: Twenty-five.
>
> Edwards: At the time you were struck how many of the boilers were in fact fired?
> Turner: Nineteen.
>
> Edwards: Was it a matter within your discretion, or was it in consequence of orders from your owners that you bad only nineteen of your boilers fired?
> Turner: Orders of the owners.
>
> Edwards: So that at that time if you had thought it the right thing to keep full speed ahead you could not have attained anywhere the maximum speed of 24 to 25 knots?
> Turner: No; 21.

Captain Turner

Donald MacMaster, representing Canadian interests, also had some questions about this issue.

"MacMaster: On the morning of the 7th May were you aware that you were in a danger zone?
Turner: I was.

MacMaster: And that you might possibly be subject to a torpedo attack?
Turner: Yes.

MacMaster: Did you give any special instructions or take any special precautions with a view to observing whether submarines where in the neighborhood on the morning of the 7th May?
Turner: I did. I gave orders to the engineers in case I rang full speed ahead to give her extra speed.

MacMaster: Did you give orders to look out for submarines?
Turner: The look-outs were already doubled."

These precautions would prove completely insufficient on May 7, 1915.

"A Million-Ton Hammer"

"Without any warning a German submarine fired a torpedo at the Lusitania and she was struck between the third and fourth funnels. There is evidence that there was a second and perhaps a third torpedo fired, and the ship sank within 20 minutes…there was no possibility under the circumstances of making any immediate preparation to save the lives of the passengers on board…the course adopted by the German Government was not only contrary to International law and the usages of war, but was contrary to the dictates of civilization and humanity; and to have sunk the passengers under those circumstances and under the conditions that I have stated meant in the eye, not only of our law but of every other law that I know of in civilized countries, a deliberate attempt to murder the passengers on board that ship." - Sir Edward Carson

"It sounded like a million-ton hammer hitting a steam boiler a hundred feet high." – A passenger on the *Lusitania*

Around 11:00 a.m. on May 7, the British Admiralty issued a warning for ships near the coast: "U-boats active in southern part of Irish Channel. Last heard of twenty miles south of Coningbeg Light Vessel." This warning was due in part to the fact that a German submarine, U-20, had fired torpedoes at several ships in the area the day before, sinking two of them. Around 1:00 p.m., ships in the area received another warning: "Submarine five miles south of Cape Clear proceeding west when sighted at 10:00 am." Unfortunately, that warning was inaccurate, and it also had the effect of making the *Lusitania*'s captain think it had already passed a German submarine.

A picture of German submarines at Kiel, with U-20 second from left

By the morning of May 7, the *Lusitania* had already started taking noticeable precautions, including using depth soundings to try detecting enemy U-boats. It had slowed down due to heavy fog in the morning, but as the fog cleared closer to noon, the *Lusitania* picked its speed back up to 18 knots (20 miles per hour).

As fate would have it, the *Lusitania* would be sighted by the same German submarine, U-20, that sank a couple of ships the day before, and one of the reasons the two crossed paths is because the German submarine was low on fuel and torpedoes and was thus heading for home. Still, with 3 torpedoes left, U-20's commander, Walther Schwieger, could target at least one more ship. His first attempted target, the cruiser *Juno*, passed the U-boat around noon but was traveling fast and zigzagging to make it harder for a submarine to target the ship. As a result, the U-20 never got a shot off at the cruiser.

Schwieger

Shortly before 1:30 p.m., the U-20 sighted a large steamer and submerged in order to advance toward it. The submarine began to tail its target, but by moving at 18 knots, the *Lusitania* could move faster than the U-boat, and no merchant ship or ocean liner moving faster than 15 knots had ever been sunk by a submarine. While it was not moving near its top speed, the *Lusitania* could still outrun the submarine, and given its course, Schwieger thought for a time that his U-20 would never get close enough to actually fire a torpedo at the *Lusitania*.

Of course, the *Lusitania*'s advantage in speed could only help if Captain Turner and the crew knew of the location of the submarine, but nobody on board even knew one was present. As a result, less than an hour after U-20 spotted the ship, a change in the *Lusitania*'s course brought it into range for a torpedo attack. Around 2:10 p.m., with his submarine less than half a mile away from the steamer, Schwieger ordered a torpedo to be fired at the target. He wrote in his submarine's log, "Torpedo hits starboard side right behind the bridge. An unusually heavy detonation takes place with a very strong explosive cloud. The explosion of the torpedo must have been followed by a second one [boiler or coal or powder?]... The ship stops immediately and heels over to starboard very quickly, immersing simultaneously at the bow... the name Lusitania becomes visible in golden letters." Raimund Weisbach, U-20's torpedo officer, also indicated his surprise at the extent of the explosion and the fact that the *Lusitania*'s forecastle (the foremost section of the upper deck forward of the mast) was already below water in less than 10 minutes.

A depiction of where the torpedo hit the ship and the damage caused by the explosion

This German depiction of the explosion incorrectly has the torpedo hitting the port side instead of the starboard side

A more accurate depiction of the *Lusitania* listing to its starboard side as it sank

The torpedo that struck the *Lusitania* was traveling at a depth of only 3 meters, making it possible to notice on board the steamer. Joseph Casey, a fireman on the ship, was one of the extra watchmen Turner ordered to keep a look out for submarines, and while he never saw U-20 itself, he recognized the torpedo. Turner later asserted, "We were given instructions how to recognize a torpedo when it was coming through the water. ... [I was] on the starboard side between the after-end of the engineers' quarters and the commencement of the second class cabins. There was another shipmate of mine and me looking at a passenger fixing a trunk up, and this shipmate says to me, 'Joe, what's that?' I immediately looked to the forward end on the starboard side and I saw two white streaks approaching the ship; one seemed to be travelling quicker than the other. At the beginning I thought there was only one, but as they approached the ship they opened outwards and the after one seemed to strike the ship either forward or near the center of No.2 funnel, and a white flash came and an explosion. There seemed to be two explosions but they were like together. ... [Later] when we were getting ready to go down the rope to go over the side aft, there was this streak of a third torpedo coming from a diagonal direction. On the starboard side. It was fired from the forward end on the starboard side, not the same as the others in a straight line, but in a diagonal line."

A British depiction shows a second torpedo hitting the *Lusitania* near the hole left by the first

A diagram showing where the (alleged) two torpedoes hit the *Lusitania*

As Casey's testimony suggests, there would be a subsequent debate over how many torpedoes had been fired. Casey insisted that there were at least 3 torpedoes fired by the U-boat, with the first two hitting and the third missing, but this is contradicted by Schwieger's account. In fact, as the *Lusitania* was in the process of sinking, Schwieger wrote down, "It looks as if the ship will stay afloat only for a very short time. [I gave order to] dive to 25 metres and leave the area seawards. I couldn't have fired another torpedo into this mass of humans desperately trying to save themselves."

Regardless of the number of torpedoes fired, most of the passengers had no idea what was going on until they felt the sudden lurch in the ship and heard the explosion, and even then, most did not know what had actually happened until they were on the lifeboats and the situation was explained to them. Reverend Clark described how the impact had thrown him to the ground: "I had come up from lunch in the lift and had gone up to the smoking room, and then, walking through the smoke room, got on to what is called the verandah. Outside the smoking room in the open air, and looking straight aft, and I was talking to an American there when the explosion took place. I did not see the torpedo, but I saw the impact, and the immediate result of the impact saw that it shook the vessel, as far as I could make out, from stem to stern, and I saw a quantity of water at once pouring down. I suppose it had been thrown up by the force of the explosion, and was coming back again, and almost immediately it seemed to me that the list to starboard started. There was a violent explosion along with the impact. I should find it very difficult to describe, because it was only momentary. I do not think I can say that I saw any smoke or anything of that sort. I felt the impact. I thought at first that it was a mine that we had struck, as I did not see the torpedo."

John Freeman, a Second Class passenger, was relaxing on deck with his wife but did not see the cause of the explosion. He discussed the initial shock and confusion: "We were sitting on the promenade deck looking at the coast of Ireland and there was this explosion. It seemed to me to be in front near the first funnel and I said to my wife, 'that is a mine' - thinking we were running on to a mine, I did not think that we should be torpedoed without any warning. We stood looking, and immediately there was a second explosion, and that was followed by hot water and steam, and it seemed to me that there were cinders as well. The second explosion took place near to the first one, and that caused a little confusion and alarm, and we stepped into the lounge to get out of the way of the steam and hot water. The second lunch was on, and the passengers came rushing up from the dining saloon, and they had just started lowering the boats. ... As soon as we crossed the gangway the people went up towards the port side almost every one of them, and I said to my wife 'We will go the other way,' and we lost our foothold immediately going down from the gangway of the vessel, and we slid down the side of the vessel. I saw about half-way down the first class promenade deck some sailors preparing to lower the boat. I thought they seemed to know their business and I noticed, that they were regular seamen, at least so it seemed to me from their jerseys. We got our feet again but the list was so great that we fell down again although we were only walking on the promenade deck, but I held on to the railing and supported my wife and got her into the boat."

While most passengers only knew that something dramatic had happened, Theodore Diamandis had the dubious honor of being one of the few passengers to see U-20. His testimony would prove crucial in the investigation surrounding the attack: "Myself and two friends of mine, two Greeks, went down and we could not get second class cabins, and we were obliged to take third class cabins. At the time she was struck we had finished lunch about half-past one, and I sat about 20 or 25 minutes talking to my friends, and then I thought of going round to have a shave in the second class. On my arrival at the barber's shop, about 30 or 40 yards on the other side, she was struck immediately. After she was struck I ran aft towards the First Class, when I went up on the top deck, and when the *Lusitania* was turning towards the land, then I saw the periscope of the submarine just disappearing. I should say about 300 yards [away]. ... Well, when I was going round to the port side and when I went upstairs on to the port deck, the *Lusitania* had then practically turned a semicircle toward the shore and from the port side you could then see the periscope from there. ... I have no experience of periscopes, but I have seen them. I know what the conning tower is. It is the larger part of the submarine. ... If it was the conning tower that the people went down into the submarine, that is what I call the conning tower."

For his part, Captain Turner had years of experience at sea, including some time spent training in naval warfare. Therefore, he was able to provide more details of the incident, including what he did in response to the first explosion: "The officer called out 'There is a torpedo coming, sir,' and I went across to the starboard side and saw the wake, and there was immediately an explosion and the ship took a heavy list. [On] the starboard side. A big volume of smoke and steam came up between the third and fourth funnels, counting from forward-I saw that myself. I saw a streak like the wake of a torpedo."

Although the *Lusitania* ended up sinking much faster than anyone expected, including the German submarine crew, there was an initial hope that it might stay above water for awhile. Albert Arthur Bestwick, a Junior Third Officer on the *Lusitania*, explained, "I heard an explosion. I was in the officers' smoke room at the time, and I went out on the bridge and I saw the track of a torpedo. It seemed to be fired in a line with the bridge, and it seemed to strike the ship between the second and third funnels, as far as I could see. Then I heard the order given 'hard-a-starboard' and I heard Captain Turner saying 'lower the boats down level to the rail,' and I went to my section of boats. My boat station was No. 10 on the port side. That was my individual boat; my section was from 2 to 10. I started to get No. 10 lowered down to the rail, but it landed on the deck. Captain Anderson was there beside me and he said: 'Go to the bridge and tell them they are to trim her with the port tanks.' I made my way to the bridge and sung out that order to Mr. Heppert, the second officer. He repeated it and I came back again and No. 10 boat was on the deck. We tried to push it out, but we could not do it. [The ship] had a big list to starboard on her. … Captain Anderson was there beside me and I took most of my orders from him. I thought when we trimmed her with the port tanks she might right herself a little bit. She went on listing for about 10 minutes I should say. Then she seemed to rectify the list a little bit. … When she rectified herself a little bit it gave us encouragement and we thought she might come up altogether or it might give us a better chance."

Since the *Lusitania* was only 15 miles from shore at that moment, Turner's first thought was that if he pushed the ship's engines, he could speed to land before the vessel sank. This was often possible with larger ships because a small hole would not allow enough water in to sink them immediately. However, he quickly realized that was not an option: "I headed her for the land to see if I could make the land. [I] ordered the boats to be lowered down to the rails, to get the women and children in first. [I] put her head on to the land, and then I saw she had a lot of way on her and was not sinking, so I put her full speed astern, to take the way off her. … [I realized] that the engines were out of commission."

Meanwhile, First Officer Arthur Jones was dealing with his own crisis. He was one of only a few stewards present in a large room of passengers who were quickly flying into a panic. He later related his experience: "Well, when we were struck there were about 100 people lunching in the saloon, and the moment she was struck of course we all got up and they preceded me out through both doors. I was about the last man to come out of the saloon. It was as I was passing through the door that I issued this order, 'Close the ports if any are open.' ... I simply told the people to be calm on the way up, and to be as collected as they possibly could."

Closing the porthole windows proved to be important, because as the ship immediately began to list to the side, it placed many of the windows on the starboard side under water. Had the windows not been closed and sealed, the water would have rushed in that much more quickly and sink the ship even faster. Carson explained, "The torpedo which struck the ship, ...struck her on the starboard side. That caused an immediate list on the ship, which, if it did momentarily right itself, afterwards increased, and was of such a nature...that it made the boats on the port side practically impossible to launch. Some of them I think were filled with passengers, but, as your Lordship will readily imagine, in the few moments that elapsed these boats with the list over fell in-board and some of them fell over upon some of the passengers on the deck."

Abandoning Ship

"The Lusitania was a passenger steamer and an emigrant ship as defined by Sections 267 and 268 of the Merchant Shipping Act, and as a passenger ship she had to be surveyed annually for the passengers' certificate, and as an emigrant ship, every voyage before clearance outwards. ... She also had to comply with the rules as to life-saving appliances, which had to be surveyed under the 431st section of the Act. There were also special instructions which are not statutory which were given by the Company as regards boat drills...The Lusitania held a passenger certificate enabling her to carry 400 passengers of each class, that would be 1,200 altogether, and a crew of 750 hands. She was certified to have, and had as a matter of fact, on board, 34 boats, capable of accommodating 1,950 persons. She had 32 lifebuoys and 2,325 life-jackets. ... The ship...seems in every way to have fulfilled the requirements of the law and the regulations that were laid down." - Sir Edward Carson

Unable to get his passengers to shore, Captain Turner next attempted to offload them into lifeboats, knowing that the survivors would soon be picked up if they could just stay afloat. However, he soon found there were problems with this plan as well: "I told them to hold on lowering the boats till the way was off the ship a bit, which was done. I told the staff captain to lower the boats when he thought the way was sufficiently off to allow them to be lowered. They could not very well lower them on the port side because of the heavy list [of] I should say about 15 degrees. They caught on the rail and capsized some of the people out. Some were let go on the run, and some of them fell inboard on the deck and hurt some of the passengers. I said 'All women and children into the boats first,' and I told them to lower them down to the rails."

Unlike the infamous *Titanic*, the *Lusitania* had plenty of lifeboats, and the maritime rules passed following the loss of the former guaranteed that there would be more than enough lifeboats to hold both the passengers and the crew. However, getting the passengers into them proved to be more difficult than anyone had anticipated. Robert Cairns, a passenger from First Class, later complained, "As a matter of fact had it not been for the passengers the [lifeboat] would never have been in the water at all; it was entirely owing to the passengers. I am pretty strong and I got right into the center, and I went back five or six paces, and I said to the others, 'The moment I rush the boat to the center, push like wild' and we were just able to get the boat over, and then I got all the women and children into the boat. I said 'women and children must go into the boat first and men afterwards.' ... She commenced to leak immediately, and there were five or six gentlemen with their hats doing their very utmost to bale her out, and just in a few moments she was right full of water level to the sea. ... When I saw the boat was level with the sea, and everyone, of course, was expecting the boat to go down every minute; I am a very good swimmer, and I jumped out immediately, and I was followed by another passenger. I had been swimming for about a minute and a half, and I had turned round to look at the boat, and the boat had gone down, capsized, with the keel upwards. All had gone down with it with the exception of two or three who were hanging on to the keel."

Though several passengers would subsequently complain that the officers and seamen alike were poorly trained and inefficient, it's only fair to note that most of the crewmen were trying to do their best under almost impossible circumstances; after all, they had never trained in launching lifeboats off of a ship that was nearly on its side in the water. Moreover, Diamandis recalled seeing lifeboats being launched in an orderly fashion: "I crossed the boat deck to the starboard side. ... There were three boats in that pat just swung in the davits and they were lowering them down and there was an officer there attending to it...giving instructions to the crew to help the people. ... I did not see any stewards, but on the deck where I was there was an officer giving instructions, and there were two or three people helping the women and children into the boats."

Naturally, no matter how trained the crew was, the attack was so sudden and violent that there was more panic than order throughout the ship. One passenger, James Baker, described some of the bedlam that many passengers experienced: "I was in my cabin, and when I got up they were lowering - I could not tell you the number-the boats opposite the leading room on the port side. I remained on the port side the whole time. I think-I am sure it was opposite the reading room, and I saw that boat run away because the man at the bows could not hold the falls. At the stern the rope fouled and left the boat bows in the water, and at an angle of about 45 degrees. There was a young officer in the water when I looked over. I did not see the start of lowering the boat, but when I looked over to see what had happened, there was a young officer trying to climb into the bows. The stern post had been wrenched away from the sides, so that when the boat did get into the water she could not possibly keep afloat. I know there was a bit of a list. When I got on to the deck there was a greater list than later on. The ship appeared to me to gradually right herself, because when I got to the second boat we were able to shove the boat out and had got her clear when we got orders to clear the boats, all women to come out."

Baker then went on to describe how the atmosphere of the ship's deck quickly broke out in chaos, due largely to the fact that the *Lusitania* was going down so fast. Discussing his efforts to help load a lifeboat on the port side of the ship, he continued, "We had filled her with women and children and we were trying to shove her out, the list having brought the boat in. We stood on the collapsible boat and tried to shove her out, and while we were attempting to do it the list was so great that the number of men there at the time could not do it. We called for more men; we had not much purchase as we were standing on top of the collapsible boat, but finally we got steady and with one shove got her clear and lowered her a foot or so, when the order came 'Stop lowering the boat. Clear the boat,' and we got everyone out."

Having realized that there was little more he could do where he was, Baker decided to go to another part of the ship and offer his services there: "I came then to very nearly the smoke room and they were at work launching a boat there; but as there seemed to be plenty of men, I started on the collapsible boat and did not attempt to help with the third boat. I heard it run away and collapse and smash up like a matchbox. May I say with regard to the second boat, while that was being lowered I came to the conclusion that there were not enough men in the boat to help shove her off the side as she ran down. I made it five men, but I will not swear to it. When I saw the boats going down and they could not hold them, I realized that it was a question of moments. I looked round to see what was being done with the collapsible boats, and I could not see one being got ready nor the canvas tops taken off, so with a penknife I cut one clear and was working on a second when I saw the water coming."

Others, despairing of finding a place on a lifeboat, began to prepare to go in the water, which obviously required donning a lifebelt. Somewhat surprisingly, many of the passengers never even tried to put theirs on, hoping instead to find a place on a lifeboat, but Reverend Clark decided it would be wise to take the time to find a life preserver to put on. He recalled, "I waited for a minute, and then I went down to my cabin on the D deck, [but there] was no lifebelt properly so-called, it was a sort of jacket. I believe it was called Boddy's Patent Jacket. ... [Then] went first to the port side. My cabin was on the starboard side but I groped my way back with very great difficulty…and I got first on to the port side for a moment, and I saw a man from a great height throw himself into the water and come down what seemed to me to be a fearful smash, and I saw another boat which was half lowered and the falls then seemed to get jammed. …A great number of people in that boat were spilled into the water, and I walked back then to the starboard side. … Eventually I got into a boat on the starboard side. … Well, when we got into the boat two of the funnels were hanging over that side and threatening to smash the boats up. I attempted to get into a boat before, but there was a woman with a child in the boat, and she was afraid of me, perhaps, jumping near her, and she screamed to me not to jump, and so I went on to what I imagined to be the last boat there. … We were so tightly packed that it was impossible to move the oars at first, and I thought the funnels would come down."

Not everyone who went back to his room to grab a life preserver was so fortunate. John Freeman, a Second Class Passenger, discovered something very eerie when he went below decks: "When I went to deck 'E' it was in darkness owing to the electric light being out, apart from a little light which came in from the port-holes on the port side of the vessel. The starboard side was entirely in darkness. I did not realize at the time that the vessel was under water, but these port-holes normally are just above the water-line."

Unlike the rumors that plagued the *Titanic*, there were no accusations among those housed in steerage that they were prevented from getting off the ship. Indeed, Joseph Frankum described how he and his family made their escape: "We were all having a cup of tea for'ard, just after getting our baggage ready for shore… something went bang. I knew what it was immediately. The vessel at once heeled over to starboard, and my little boy turned and said, 'What's that, Daddy?' I didn't answer him… As soon as the explosion occurred, I gripped my two boys while my wife took charge of the little girl… I wouldn't wait to get lifebelts, as I was afraid we should get trapped below."

Instead, they quickly made their way to the upper deck. Frankum continued, "In the hurry, I dropped my little boy who fell about six feet, but I picked him up again and we made our way towards one of the boats… I pushed the wife and kiddies into a boat and said, 'You stay there while I try and get a lifebelt… I shall be alright.' Then I made for the second cabin saloon and got a couple of the lifebelts. Remembering that my people were already in the boat, I said, 'Here, old man, take this.' [to a man who did not have a lifebelt]. When I got back to the deck, I found the missus and the children had got out of the boat. The steamer had got a heavy list, but just then she steadied a bit and I thought she might right herself… She started to heel over again. I said to my wife 'Oh my God, it's all over. Get back into the lifeboat again.'"

By then, it was too late, and the water was coming up over the deck. Frankum explained his futile attempt to hold onto his family: "I hoped that as she sank the lifeboat might rise in her chocks, but whether it did or not I don't know, for the next instant I was wrenched from my hold and hurled into the water… I stuck to my wife and children as long as I could, but as we sank, we were separated… I was sucked down very deep but came to the surface again. I could find no traces of my wife nor any of the children." At that point, he managed to get himself into another lifeboat: "A young gentleman who was on the boat tried to comfort me for the loss of my family, and while he was so engaged a man's body floated alongside us. The young gentleman picked up an oar and lifted the head of the dead man. 'Good God,' he cried, 'It's my own father.' And then I had to comfort him."

In the end, Frankum would learn that only one of his three children, his son Francis, had survived.

Total Loss

"The Track of Lusitania," a 1915 illustration depicting bodies and survivors in the wake of the sinking

"The total crew was 702, made up of deck department 77, engineering department 314, stewards 306, the orchestra 5; that made 702. Of these, there were 677 males and 25 females. 397 males and 16 females were lost; therefore, the total loss of the crew was 413; 280 males and 9 females were saved. Those figures make up the 702. The total passengers were 1,257, made up of saloon passengers 290, second -cabin passengers 600, third- cabin passengers 367, making a total of 1,257. Of these there were 688 adult males, 440 adult females, 51 male children, and 39 female children, and 39 infants. The number of passengers lost was 785, and the number saved 472. Of the 129 children, 94 were lost and 35 saved." - Sir Edward Carson

Given the rapid chain of events, most of the passengers on board the *Lusitania* never even had a chance to make it to a lifeboat or even get back to their rooms and don lifebelts. According to First Officer Jones, "After I had lowered No. 15 in the water I then went down the fall myself a few seconds afterwards, and the boat deck was level with the water. A matter of 15 seconds; it was not half a minute. Well, she started with her head to starboard and then she went down by the head herself, and, I take it, as far as I can judge, she upended herself until her nose touched the bottom and then she sank down herself. I should say she had an angle of about 30 degrees from the perpendicular."

To a world that had barely recovered from the shocking loss of the Titanic a few years earlier, the loss of the *Lusitania* came as a terrible blow. While the death tolls in each disaster were nearly equal, there were aspects of the *Lusitania's* sinking that made it so much more offensive to the human psyche. For one thing, the ship went down very fast, going from sailing on the sea to sitting at the bottom 300 feet below in less than 20 minutes. This meant that those who did survive had little time to even come to terms with what was happening. Furthermore, there was the fact that the *Lusitania* was deliberately sunk, not the result of a tragic but accidental disaster.

Even for those who made it to lifeboats, there was still plenty of danger, and many who thought they had reached the safety of the small crafts were instead suddenly plunged to their deaths. David Alfred Thomas, one of the passengers from First Class, later complained, "I would say that there was no kind of organization, but there was certainly panic five or ten minutes after the boat was struck, and I do not think the order of the captain, 'women and children first,' was obeyed by a very large number of the crew. They looked after themselves first - they took care to save themselves first - in fact I met two or three of them afterwards, and they were boasting about it at Queenstown. I know at the time the first boat sank - it is not direct evidence - there were very few women and children in the boat that I got into. The first boat on the port side was let down so badly that the whole of the passengers and crew that were in it fell into the water - there were very few women in that. ... I was going to say that of course the Court can ascertain for themselves probably the figures of those saved, the different classes, women and children, and the first, second, and third class passengers and crew. With regard to the first boat, I was told by a number of people in the first boat that it was let down more rapidly than the others, that was on the port side, and the whole of those in the boat were plunged into the water, and my daughter, who was close by me, told me that there were very few in that boat and that there were not more than half a dozen children in that boat."

Another factor that made the sinking of the *Lusitania* shocking to the entire world was the many nationalities represented among the victims. While most of the passengers on board were from Great Britain, Canada or the United States, there were people lost from a total of 20 different countries, covering every populated continent in the world. Many of the losses were also infamous because of the popularity or notoriety of so many of those killed. For instance, the popular opera singer Millie Baker, then only 27 years old, lost her life. The American playwright and actor Charles Klein was drowned, along with producer Charles Frohman and novelist Justus Forman. The three were on their way back to England from America, where they had been looking for a backer for a new play based on Forman's novel, *The Hyphen*. Forman's obituary summed up his life and work: "When the *Lusitania* sank, finis was written to his last story, and now his career is as a tale that is told. No account of his final great adventure has come back from the scene of his tragic close. Those to whom his coming was a pleasure and who will never again welcome him, can only surmise that he met his end calmly and without dismay or fear, as an American gentleman should, and that came to his comfort and support that dominating vital sense which characterized his life and will ever be associated with his memory in the mind of his friends. He must have died as one who goes forth expectantly and wholly unafraid in quest of lands unknown, but filled with possibilities of happy venturing."

Forman

There were hundreds of heart-wrenching stories, such as that of the Aitken family: James, 57, Jarvie, 32, and James Jarvie, 2. They were traveling back to England after burying Jarvie's young wife, Grace, in Canada, and all three generations went down together. Then there were the Allen's, consisting of mother Marguerite and her two daughters, Anna and Gwen. When the ship went down, the girls fell into the ocean, and Marguerite then jumped in with them, crying out that they should all die together. Instead, she survived and lived on with the memory of her two children dying before her eyes. Mr. and Mrs. Walter Bailey drowned along with their daughter, Ivy, leaving behind their son, 14 year old Albert Victor.

One of the strangest losses was that of Lindon Bates, a well-known author and philanthropist, not because of the way he died but because of what happened when his brother tried to claim his body. According to one article, "Lindell T. Bates, son of Lindon W. Bates of New York, Vice Chairman of the American Commission for the Relief of Belgium, was arrested at Kinsale yesterday on a charge of espionage while searching for the body of his brother, Lindon W. Bates, Jr., who is believed to have perished on the *Lusitania*. Newton B. Knox, an American mining engineer, who was with Mr. Bates, was taken into custody at the same time. 'The Sergeant who made the arrests accused them of being officers of a German submarine. After being taken before a Captain they were detained at the barracks half an hour, until United States Consul Frost, at Queenstown, vouched for their innocence. Their search of the coast revealed no trace of the body of L. W. Bates, Jr.'"

Francis Bertram Jenkins, a First Class Passenger, told the harrowing story of how one woman, Mrs. Crichton, lost her life, and how he barely survived: "She was partly in the boat, I was standing with one foot on the deck of the *Lusitania* and one foot on the lifeboat, when one of the ropes broke, or the sailors loosed their hold, and the thing collapsed and went into the water. I seemed to go down a long way, and when I came up I was under the boat. It was bottom upwards. Then I saw an open port hole about two feet above me, and I clutched it but could not hold on. Then I saw a rope hanging down, which I got hold of and some twenty others too [sic] hold of it. We seemed to be sinking and some could not swim. I let go and then I saw a champagne case which I swam to but let go, and then swam for an oar. Then I saw a long piece of wood some distance ahead of me, which I swam for and in an exhausted condition reached it."

Another aspect of the tragedy that broke the hearts of many family members was the fact that so many of the bodies were never recovered, and many of those that were recovered proved unidentifiable. Albert Blicke was a passenger in First Class who was never seen again after the ship sank, and his wife, in a desperate appeal to find his body and gain some closure, circulated this description to anyone she thought might have seen him:

"Albert Blicke

Age about: 53. Height: about 5 feet 6 inches. Eyes: blue. Hair: sandy and thin. On abdomen, 2 scars from operation. Clothes: Suit, dark material. In the pocket, wallet with gold mountings containing English money and papers. Little notebooks in pockets. Watch and chain, gold and platinum. On watch is mongram, A.C.B. Ring, turquoise and two diamonds. Underwear: Linen mesh, short and drawers. Abdominal belt, silk hose, caught up with gilt clasps. Shirt marked on sleeve by monogram 'A.C.B.' and back of shirt marked 'Sulka & Co., Paris & New York.' Cuff buttons set with light blue sapphires. Collar, white turnover. Neck tie, dark. Stick pin, emeralds surrounded with diamonds."

Another terrible story surrounded Cecelia Owen and her family. On that fateful day, she was in her Second Class cabin watching her young niece, Bessie, while her brother and sister-in-law,

Alfred and Elizabeth Smith, had lunch. Her own sons, 10 year old Reginald and 6 year old Ronald, were playing on the starboard deck with her other niece, 6 year old Helen. They were supposed to return to the cabin by noon but instead came by to plead that they be allowed to continue playing. Charmed by their request, Owen granted them another half-hour of play, a decision she would regret for the rest of her life.

Just moments after the boys ran back to their game, the torpedo hit, and upon hearing the explosion, Owen took her niece Bessie in her arms and rushed upstairs to find her boys. On the way, she ran into the Smith's, who gratefully took their daughter from her and then rushed off to look for Helen. Owen continued looking for her boys and calling their names until she was picked up and forced into a lifeboat. No sooner had it been lowered than it capsized and dumped her into the ocean. A strong swimmer, she was able to make her way to another boat which was also on its side. She clung to it until she was rescued a few hours later.

Once she reached land, she was given the tragic news that she was the only member of her family to make it out alive, but then came a small piece of good news. A little girl calling herself Helen Smith was in a nearby hospital, and when Owen rushed to her, she was greeted by a child's voice crying out, "There's my auntie."

As soon as the shock began to wear off, Owen wrote her brother, Arthur, who had not come with the family on the trip: "I will try and write a few words to ease your mind & my own. You know of my dreadful trouble. I am thankful to God I am alive & no limbs are broken. My darlings are gone, also dear Alf, Bessie, Baby. Helen & myself left…I swam for my life & was picked up by some fellow pulling me on a collapsable boat (I can't spell today) I had a terrible experience. I am thankful I have my mind also limbs which are bruised all over. I am under a doctor's care and feel better than I did, but oh, my heart aches and will always. My dear boys were with me five minutes before it happened but I never saw them again…Oh Arthur, this is a dreadful blow. Everything I possess is gone and my darlings as well. Also our dear Alf and his lot…I am trying to be brave. God will still give me strength to overcome this as he saved me for some purpose.

    Your broken hearted sister.

    CE"

In the hours that followed the loss of the *Lusitania*, small vessels from up and down the coast of Liverpool poured into the area to rescue the living, but given how quickly the ship sank and the fact that the water was only about 50 degrees Fahrenheit, it was far too late for many who fell into the water and couldn't scramble onto a lifeboat or a large piece of debris. Even with the quick response, only 300 corpses were recovered, and nearly a quarter of those couldn't be identified either.

People later told stories of being picked up by every type of boat from small fishing vessels to large navy trawlers. In all, 761 people were pulled from the water, about a third of them members of the crew. This does not necessarily reflect any sort of selfishness on their part as much as it does the benefit of their experience with the sea. 94 of the 129 children on board that day drowned, not because anyone was negligent in trying to save them but because there was not enough time for the preference typically given to women and children in a disaster situation. 35 of the children lost were infants, too young to even try making it to safety.

Bjørn Christian Tørrissen's picture of a memorial marking a mass grave for *Lusitania* victims in Cobb, Ireland

Certain Statements

> # MEN OF LEICESTERSHIRE
> ## AVENGE THE
> # LUSITANIA
> ## HOW TO DO IT!
> For every Man, Woman and Child lost 10 Men should join.
>
> **JOIN THE 10TH BATTALION LEICESTERSHIRE REGIMENT**
> 21, HUMBERSTONE GATE.
>
> **14 DAYS LEAVE AT HOME ON JOINING**
> PAY AND ALLOWANCES 3/- PER DAY WHILST ON LEAVE.

A British recruiting poster in the wake of the disaster

A French paper's photographs of *Lusitania* survivors and victims

"Certain statements have been made which have become public, and certain allegations have been made as between the German Government and America; Notes have passed between them, and it is not inconvenient that I should tell…the statement which the United States have made as regards the requirements of their laws before the steamship Lusitania sailed for Liverpool." - Sir Edward Carson

"[A] deed for which a Hun would blush, a Turk be ashamed, and a Barbary pirate apologize." - *The Nation*

From the moment the *Lusitania* was struck by a torpedo and two explosions ripped through its hull, Germany insisted that the ship was illegally smuggling weapons from America to Britain and thus carrying "contraband of war." German spokesman Dr Bernhard Dernburg also noted that the *Lusitania* "was classed as an auxiliary cruiser," and the fact that it was in a war zone made it a justifiable target regardless of the passengers on board. Secretary of State William Jennings Bryan, who later resigned due to opposing American involvement in the war, seemingly echoed some of the Germans' positions when he suggested to President Wilson that "ships carrying contraband should be prohibited from carrying passengers … it would be like putting women and children in front of an army."

However, in its official response, Wilson's administration reacted indignantly to such allegations. A note passed on to the Germans began by reviewing the charges Germany made against the country: "Your Excellency's Note, in discussing the loss of American lives resulting from the sinking of the steamship 'Lusitania,' adverts at some length to certain information which the Imperial German Government has received with regard to the character and outfit of that vessel, and Your Excellency expresses the fear that this information has not been brought to the attention of the United States. It is stated that the *Lusitania* was undoubtedly equipped with masked guns, that she was supplied with trained gunners with special ammunition, that she was transporting troops from Canada, that she was carrying cargo not permitted under the laws of the United States to a vessel also carrying passengers, and that she was serving, in virtual effect, as an auxiliary to the naval forces of Great Britain."

From there, the letter went on to make it perfectly clear that not only were German's accusations false, they were also insulting, especially in light of the number of American lives lost and the fact that no state of war existed between the United States and Germany at the time: "Fortunately these are matters concerning which the Government of the United States is in a position to give the Imperial German Government official information. Of the facts alleged in Your Excellency's Note, if true, the Government of the United States would have been bound to take official cognizance. Performing its recognized duty as a neutral Power and enforcing its national laws, it was its duty to see to it that the *Lusitania* was not armed for offensive action, that she was not serving as a transport, that she did not carry cargo prohibited by the statutes of the United States, and that if, in fact, she was a naval vessel of Great Britain she should not receive a clearance as a merchantman. It performed that duty. It enforced its statutes with scrupulous vigilance through its regularly constituted officials, and it is able therefore to assure the Imperial German Government that it has been misinformed."

Finally, the letter hinted at actions to come. Many Americans had already been clamoring for the United States to join the war, and the loss of the *Lusitania* would set into motion a series of events that would soon see America join World War I as one of Germany's most ardent foes: "If the Imperial German Government should deem itself to be in possession of convincing evidence that the officials of the Government of the United States did not perform these duties with thoroughness, the Government of the United States sincerely hopes that it will submit that evidence for consideration. Whatever may be the contentions of the Imperial German Government regarding the carriage of contraband of war on board the *Lusitania* or regarding the explosion of that material by a torpedo, it need only be said that in the view of this Government these contentions are irrelevant to the question of the legality of the methods used by the German naval authorities in sinking the vessel."

A cartoon depicting America's disapproval over the German sinking of ships like the *Lusitania*

When America formally protested the action, German Kaiser Wilhelm II wrote his own comments in the margins of the complaint, including "utterly impertinent," "outrageous," and "this is the most insolent thing in tone and bearing that I have had to read since the Japanese note last August." However, the Kaiser also understood the diplomatic damage Germany had suffered as a result of the sinking of the *Lusitania* and placed restrictions on the naval warfare to placate the United States, at least for a time. Although Americans were understandably outraged and newspapers thunderously denounced the attack, President Wilson made clear that he still would not join the war in a speech given on May 10: "There is such a thing as a man being too proud to fight. There is such a thing as a nation being so right that it does not need to convince others by force that it is right."

Not surprisingly, the British government supported America's response, and conspiracy theories have continued to accuse the British of either instigating or at least passively allowing the loss of the *Lusitania* in order to garner international sympathy and draw the United States into the war. It's also no coincidence that the man usually accused by the conspiracy theories is Winston Churchill, who was First Lord of the Admiralty when the *Lusitania* sunk. Similar conspiracy theories have accused Churchill of knowingly withholding information about the impending Japanese attack on Pearl Harbor from the Roosevelt administration to guarantee American entry into World War II. Although he couldn't possibly have plotted the *Lusitania*'s demise, Churchill would try to make a scapegoat out of Captain Turner in the aftermath of the disaster to avoid having the tragedy tarnish the government.

Regardless of the conspiracy theories, Sir Edward Carson echoed the Americans and denied the German allegations: "May I say here, at the outset, that that being a statement of the enforcement of the Regulations under Statutes at the port of departure, New York, our evidence here fully confirms the statement that was made. There was no such outfitting of the vessel as is alleged and fancied or invented by the German Government; and your Lordship will have the fullest evidence of that from the witnesses we will call in confirmation of what was said by the United States Government."

Some would later assert that the ship was made a bigger target because it was not traveling fast enough, and this was offered as evidence that the crew was failing to do all that it could to avoid being targeted. This also played into the idea that England was setting the ship up for destruction. However, Carson had an answer for that as well, noting that "the average maximum at which she had travelled from New York was about 21 knots, and a question will arise as to whether the captain was right in travelling at the time at 18 knots. I ought, further, to mention this, because it is a matter that concerns the owners, that out of 25 boilers they had in use all through the voyage only 19…the owners of the ship, the Cunard Company, say is, that in consequence of the war and the decrease of passenger traffic between America and this country, they had determined, not merely as regards this ship, but as regards other ships engaged in the traffic, and on other voyages of this ship, to use only the 19 boilers with a view to economy, having regard to the passenger traffic which they anticipated. That enabled them to do with about three-fourths of the coal that would be ordinarily used, and enabled them to save a certain amount of labor. Whether that was right or wrong we shall probably have to inquire somewhat into. But it is right to say that even with the boiler accommodation which was in use, I understand, that the *Lusitania*, making 21 knots, would be a faster ship that any other of the large trans-Atlantic liners which convey passengers from one country to another."

There was also the matter of how the crew functioned during the emergency, as well as the state of the gear used to lower the lifeboats. Following the ship's loss, the British government held an inquiry into its sinking. It was a unique hearing when it came to investigating a sinking, as Carson pointed out: "We know in the present case that there was no accident. We know that there was a premeditated design to murder these people on board this ship by sinking her. Everything points to that perfectly clearly and perfectly plainly...The real questions that will arise upon that are only two. The first is as to the navigation of the ship, having regard to the instructions, and the suggestions and the information from the Admiralty, and the second is as to whether everything was done that possibly could be done to save human life and alleviate human suffering after the ship had been torpedoed. ... There is one thing which I might state which I think all the witnesses concur in, that there was no panic. ...In certain circumstances of this kind, and with the number of human beings who were on board, it is not very easy to get any very accurate description of what did really happen as regards each boat, or anything of that kind. ...we shall court inquiry and evidence, as is our duty, from any other person who wishes to come forward here, and if there are complaints against either the master or the owners or the crew everybody here as I understand will have the fullest opportunity of stating it. That is one of the objects of the investigation, but as I said before, this investigation differs from all others that I know of which have been held in these wreck inquiries, because, unfortunately, the cause of the loss of life is only too clear."

The inquiry was a brief affair that lasted just five days, but during that time, the committee heard from both passengers and crewmen, all of whom agreed for the most part about why the ship sink. This led the committee to wind up its deliberations and issue a simple statement: "The Court, having carefully enquired into the circumstances of the above mentioned disaster, finds, that the loss of the said ship and lives was due to damage caused to the said ship by torpedoes fired by a submarine of German nationality whereby the ship sank. In the opinion of the Court the act was done not merely with the intention of sinking the ship, but also with the intention of destroying the lives of the people on board."

The question of whether the *Lusitania* was carrying guns or other armaments has been debated since the day the ship went down. The cargo manifest made clear that the ship was carrying rifle cartridges and empty shell casings, something the British not only admitted but conceded had been carried on the *Lusitania* throughout the war. It was only decades later that declassified documents indicated that the ship was indeed carrying over 50 tons of live ammunition from the United States to Britain. Indeed, the British government began warning divers who went to explore the wreck that there were dangerous contents down there: "Successive British governments have always maintained that there was no munitions on board the Lusitania (and that the Germans were therefore in the wrong to claim to the contrary as an excuse for sinking the ship) ... The facts are that there is a large amount of ammunition in the wreck, some of which is highly dangerous. The Treasury have decided that they must inform the salvage company of this fact in the interests of the safety of all concerned."

That said, while the Germans claimed that the secondary explosion was evidence of weaponry being hidden in the ship, explorations of the wreck have more recently led historians to believe that the secondary explosion was actually caused by an exploding boiler, not the detonation of munitions. Furthermore, it's fair to question whether the presence of the munitions truly mattered since the ship itself was not armed and posed no threat to any vessel, German or otherwise. With the possible exception of a few soldiers on leave, the ship's passengers were all civilians, so it may be better to ask whether the Germans were justified in sinking a ship full of civilians simply to keep weapons from falling into their enemies' hands. Sir Edward offered his answer, one with which most people would likely agree: "At the present moment, all I want to emphasize is that there was no warning and there was no possibility under the circumstances of making any immediate preparation to save the lives of the passengers on board. My Lord, the course adopted by the German Government was not only contrary to International law and the usages of war, but was contrary to the dictates of civilization and humanity; and to have sunk the passengers under those circumstances and under the conditions that I have stated meant in the eye, not only of our law but of every other law that I know of in civilized countries, a deliberate attempt to murder the passengers on board that ship"

A British recruitment poster that features the sinking of the *Lusitania* in the background

A British stamp that featured the *Lusitania* and asked people not to buy German goods

Mike Peel's picture of one of the *Lusitania's* propellers in Liverpool

Online Resources

Other books about the Titanic on Amazon

Other books about the Lusitania on Amazon

Further Reading

Aldridge, Rebecca (2008). *The Sinking of the* Titanic. New York: Infobase Publishing.

Burns, Greg, *Commemoration of Death: the medals of the Lusitania murders.* (August 2012), full color bleed, 194 pages.

Bailey, Thomas A. and Paul B. Ryan. *The Lusitania Disaster: An Episode in Modern Warfare and Diplomacy* (1975)

Ballard, Robert D., & Dunmore, Spencer. (1995). *Exploring the Lusitania.* New York: Warner Books.

Ballard, Robert D. (1987). *The Discovery of the* Titanic. New York: Warner Books.

Butler, Daniel Allen (2002) [1998]. *Unsinkable: the full story of the RMS Titanic.* USA: Da Capo Press.

Crosbie, Duncan; Mortimer, Sheila (2006). *Titanic: The Ship of Dreams.* New York, NY: Orchard Books.

Eaton, John P.; Haas, Charles A. (1995). Titanic*: Triumph and Tragedy.* New York: W.W. Norton & Company.

Gill, Anton (2010). *Titanic: the real story of the construction of the world's most famous ship.* Channel 4 Books.

Halpern, Samuel; Weeks, Charles (2011). "Description of the Damage to the Ship". In Halpern, Samuel. *Report into the Loss of the SS* Titanic*: A Centennial Reappraisal.* Stroud, UK: The History Press.

Hutchings, David F.; de Kerbrech, Richard P. (2011). *RMS Titanic 1909–12 (Olympic Class): Owners' Workshop Manual.* Sparkford, Yeovil: Haynes.

Layton, J. Kent (19 December 2010). *Lusitania: an illustrated biography.* Amberley Books.

Lord, Walter (2005) [1955]. *A Night to Remember.* New York: St. Martin's Griffin.

McCluskie, Tom (1998). *Anatomy of the* Titanic. London: PRC Publishing.

Mersey, Lord (1999) [1912]. *The Loss of the Titanic, 1912*. The Stationery Office.

Molony, Senan (2004). *Lusitania, an Irish Tragedy*. Mercier. p. 192.

Mowbray, Jay Henry (1912). *Sinking of the* Titanic. Harrisburg, PA: The Minter Company.

O'Sullivan, Patrick. (2000). *The Lusitania: Unraveling the Mysteries*. New York: Sheridan House.

Mitch Peeke; Steven Jones, Kevin Walsh-Johnson (31 October 2002). *The Lusitania story*. Barnsley, Yorkshire: Leo Coope (Pen and Sword books).

Preston, Diana (2002). *Wilful Murder: The sinking of the Lusitania*. London: Corgi (Transworld publishers).

Ramsay, David (3 September 2001). *Lusitania Saga and Myth*. London: Chatham Publishing.

Rasor, Eugene L. (2001). *The* Titanic*: historiography and annotated bibliography*. Westport, CT: Greenwood Publishing Group.

Sauder, Eric; Ken Marschall, Audrey Pearl Lawson Johnston (1 October 2009). *RMS Lusitania: The Ship and Her Record*. London: The History Press.

Sauder, Eric; Ken Marschall (December 1991). *RMS Lusitania: Triumph of the Edwardian Age*. Redondo Beach CA: Trans-Atlantic Deigns.

Spignesi, Stephen J. (1998). *The Complete* Titanic*: From the Ship's Earliest Blueprints to the Epic Film*. Secaucus, New Jersey: Birch Lane Press.

Ward, Greg (2012). *The Rough Guide to the* Titanic. London: Rough Guides Ltd.

Free Books by Charles River Editors

We have brand new titles available for free most days of the week. To see which of our titles are currently free, click on this link.

Discounted Books by Charles River Editors

We have titles at a discount price of just 99 cents everyday. To see which of our titles are currently 99 cents, click on this link.

CPSIA information can be obtained
at www.ICGtesting.com
Printed in the USA
LVHW081537180819
628041LV00032B/1865/P